MANAGEMENT INNOVATION

STRATEGIC TOOLS FOR DECISION MAKING

A must for all students & professionals in management

Dr. Dilip M. Sarwate | Amitabh D. Sarwate

VISHWAKARMA PUBLICATIONS VP ®

MANAGEMENT INNOVATION
STRATEGIC TOOLS FOR DECISION MAKING
First Edition - January 2016
© Author

ISBN 978-81-927132-8-1

Published by:
Vishwakarma Publications
283, Budhawar Peth, Near City Post,
Pune- 411 002.
Phone No: (020) 20261157
Email: info@vpindia.co.in
Website: www.vpindia.co.in

Cover Design
Abhishek Darekar - Vishwakarma Publications

Typeset and Layout
Chaitali Nachnekar - Vishwakarma Publications

Printed at
Repro India Limited, Mumbai

This book is dedicated to
Deepa - my dear daughter-in-law and
the wife of my co-author

PREFACE

Peter Drucker once had said that all organizations do only two things. That is, Marketing and Innovation respectively. There is no confusion on the former but there are so many connotations on the latter. The words like idea, creativity, invention, R & D and innovation are used synonymously. This obviously causes confusion in the minds of many.

This book aims at bringing the necessary clarity. The innovation could be either tangible or intangible. The iPod, iPhone, hybrid cars, plasma TV's will fall in the former category. However, concepts like core competency, product portfolio matrix and positioning will fall in the latter. This book is on Management Innovation which is mostly intangible.

In last 150 years or more, several management thinkers have done a great job in developing different tools & techniques to improve the performance of an individual as well as an organization. This knowledge is scattered over different disciplines. We felt the need to bring all of them together in one book so that the students and practitioners of management can put it to use.

This is also our tribute to the large number of innovators who showed the brilliance in developing these innovations.

The knowledge, we believe, is universal. The success lies in its effective application. Hence, the discerning readers will notice that our emphasis is more on the applications of these techniques with the help of few simple illustrations.

Innovation is something which never goes out of fashion. On the contrary, what we are noticing is that the speed of innovation needs to be improved. We will emphasize that innovation is no one's monopoly. In this book, we have one chapter on 'Social Innovation' where we have given many examples of innovation which is carried out by ordinary people. Many of them did not have the benefit of college education.

Quite a few of them come from rural parts of India. However, they displayed a passion to make improvements in the day-to-day life benefiting a common person.

It must also be noted that the cost of innovation is on the rise. It, therefore, requires a consortium approach. It will also require investment in talent. The organizations will have to create an environment which will motivate all the persons to do the needful. This will require creating 'Intrapreneurs' in the organization, eliminate red tape and allow persons to make mistakes and learn from them. If this book brings out the latent creativity in every person, this will be the success of the book.

We wrote these 20 articles on a monthly basis in the magazine "Sampada" published by Pune's prestigious Mahrattha Chamber of Commerce, Industries & Agriculture (MCCIA). We got good feedback after the release of every article. We would like to thank all these people as well as MCCIA for the encouragement.

Dilip M. Sarwate | Amitabh D. Sarwate

CONTENTS

1 | The Milestones in Management Innovation

There are thousands of organizations in India in terms of size, sector and nature of business. They are in small, medium and large-scale sector. They are in government, public, private and in cooperative sector. They are in manufacturing of engineering, consumer goods, original equipments as well as for components. They are in trading and in offering variety of services. What makes some of them great organizations while a majority of them struggle to survive? Many, unfortunately, also close down. The successful ones come out with consistent performance and offer benefits to all their stakeholders. The answer is simple. They are consistently striving for excellence. Coming out with innovations of some kind or the other, constantly, brings this difference.

However, it must be made clear that the organizations by themselves do not achieve excellence. People bring about the innovation. These people could be at any level. They are possessed with passion to bring the difference. As the cliché goes, 'successful people do not do different things, they do things differently'.

The three waves

When Alvin Toffler wrote his book 'The third wave', many people were puzzled. What about the other two waves, they asked? Toffler did give an answer to their queries. He said that some 300 years back, the world economies were affected by the 'first wave' which he called the Agriculture wave' when the world developed new methods of agriculture. That included use of hybrid seeds, lift irrigation, plant protection and many others. Then Toffler said that some 150 years back, we were affected by the 'second wave', which he called the 'industrial wave'. The organized industries came up with railroad, mining, construction, automobiles and many others. It is at this time that 'Innovation' became the name of the game. It has continued its journey unabated. In 2015, it has become of prime importance. Of course, then Toffler said that by 1970 we were engulfed in the 'third wave', which was the 'information wave'. While we were dealing with information even prior to 1970, this era was ushered in due to technological revolution of the following kind:

- The massive generation of information and limitations in managing it manually.

- Advent of the microprocessor chip which brought in the personal computers which became friendly and affordable.

- Internet and the World Wide Web (WWW), which brought in millions of web sites at your doorstep. And with it, the knowledge revolution.

The articles in this book are on 'Innovation', which started with the industrial wave. They are, more precisely on 'Management Innovation'. We will be tracing the history over last nearly 200 years.

What is innovation?

The word 'Innovation' certainly has several connotations. Particularly, when it is added with a prefix.

Innovation (def.) (noun):

Novelty, change, something new, something different

Now start adding the prefixes like product, process, operational and others to the word 'Innovation' and a different meaning will emerge. (See box)

Product innovation (few examples)

- In entertainment electronics, we started with record players, and then came spool type tape recorders, the cassette recorders, then CD players, DVD players, Walkman, I-Pods, I-Pad and then I-Phones.

- For computers, starting with electronic valves, then transistors, then IC Circuits and finally the silicon microprocessor chips (Intel 8088 to the present Pentium 4 chips).

Process innovation (few examples)

- In sugar factories, besides making sugar, production of industrial alcohol, liquors, ethanol and generating electricity from the waste material

- By cracking of naphtha, production of variety of plastic raw materials like LDPE, HDPE, PP, PVC, Polystyrene and many others

Operational innovation (few examples)

- Like containerization for transport of cargo which improves protection, avoids pilferage and results in optimum utilization of shipping space

- Like pre-cooling of grapes to 3 degrees Celsius to

> improve the preservation of the perishables, use of refrigerated containers

Difference between invention versus innovation

We have close to 24 research laboratories in the country, which come under the Council of Scientific and Industrial Research (CSIR). Then, there are large numbers of Defense Research Development Organizations (DRDO), which come under the Ministry of Defense. These research laboratories are involved more in 'inventions' than in 'innovations'. The work done is more at the laboratory level. They have massive budgets available provided by the government. Every year, they give a list of product and process inventions developed by them. However, how many of them are commercialized and meet with success will be an embarrassing question. (See box)

The authors initiated a study on "inventors" in India who were recipients of awards or honors for their inventions. The study aimed to find out how many of these award-winning inventions were commercialized and how many of them met with success. The findings were shocking. The rate of commercialization was less than 10% and the success rate was even lower than that. Does that mean we do not require inventions? What are the possible reasons for lack of commercialization? Wherein lies the problem? Is it with the inventor, lack of market acceptance, problems in raising funds to set up a business or any others?

Persons like James Watt, Thomas Alva Edison, Albert Einstein, and Madam Marie Curie were all inventors. We would not dare to call them 'innovators'. In all probability, their discoveries were put to commercial use by someone else. So how do we exactly define 'innovation'? We would suggest following factors to differentiate:

- It must be commercialized. That means put to use.
- It must be perceived by the customers as "something new'
- It must provide the users some novelty
- It must work as a change agent (see box)

Some examples of innovation

- Banks introduced Automatic Teller Machines (ATM). One may consider it as an extension of the banking services, perhaps, nothing new. But, as against the fixed timings of banks earlier, now the customer can have 24 hours of banking services. The customer perceives this as something new.

- With 'net broking' and 'de-mat accounts', gone are the days when you had to make rounds with your brokers, always had that feeling that he is taking you for a ride. It used to take months to effect the share transfer and what not. You are still dealing in shares but with innovation, the process has become much comfortable.

- Now you can do your rail, air and hotel reservation through the net. Travel has become easier with no hassles.

- Recall when did you last send a letter through the post office? The e-mail has revolutionized the communication even though the personal touch may have been lost!

What is management innovation?

Having understood the world of innovation with several illustrations, now let us add the prefix 'Management 'to the word 'Innovation'

Gary Hamel, visiting professor of strategic and international management at the London School of Business and a reputed consultant in his own right, operating from California, USA has undoubtedly been a pioneer on this subject. Along with Prof. C. K. Prahlad from University of Michigan (Ann Arbor), their book 'Competing for the future' (19995) was a best seller. The sequel of the book, which was equally noticed was 'Leading the revolution' (2000).

Definition: Management Innovation (MI) can be defined as a marked departure from traditional management principles, processes and practices or a departure from customary organizational form that significantly alter the way the work of management is performed. It develops new ways of organizing and managing business for success. It is a fact that very few individuals and organizations have given a thought for continuous management innovation. Gary Hamel and few others have set up Innovation Labs to bring in new concepts to improve management practices. The authors have set up Idea Labs to bring thinkers from all over the world for this purpose. It must be clearly understood that MI is totally different than Operational innovation.

This book will bring into focus the different MI tools, which have been developed in last 160 years or so. It will describe the tool but more importantly, with an illustration, it will explain its applicability. After all, it was Confucius the Chinese philosopher who had said 2500 years back that 'the essence of knowledge is, having it, to apply it'.

Milestones in management innovation

The development of management science over last 160 years has been fascinating. We can identify many milestones in its development. It can be divided in different schools in order to correctly understand them. Given below are the landmarks in different disciplines and pays a tribute to the pioneers.

Classical Theory

This resulted from the quest for higher productivity, creation of work standards, and professionalization of management, formal managerial training and functional organization.

1860s	Classical Organization Theory	Henry Fayol, Max Weber
1890s	Scientific Management	Fredrick W. Taylor, Henry L. Gantt, Frank & Lillian Gilbreth
1910s	Bridging Classical, Behavioral and System	Mary Parker Follet, Chester Barnard, Philip Selznick

Behavioral School

It came to the light that psychology plays a major role in the behavior of workers. The work was considered as a social activity. It came out that human relations also play a major role at the work place.

1910	Industrial Psychology	Hugo Munsterberg
1930	Human relations	Elton Mayo
	Public Administration	Lyndall Urwick
1950	Theory X, Theory Y	Douglas McGreg or
1960s	Humanism	Abraham Maslow Fredrick Herzberg
1970s	System 4	Rensis Likert
1990s	Emotional Intelligence	Daniel Goleman

Quantitative School

The subjects of statistics, mathematics, and operations research were developed for the use in organizations. This was the scientific approach to decision making and problem solving

1940s	Operations Research	P.M.S. Blackett
1950's	Systems Analysis	Norbert Wiener Russel Ackoff
1960	Decision Theory	Herbert Simon, Howard Raiffa & Schlaifer

Organizational Theories

1930's brought in the era of mass production. Henry Ford I was the pioneer in this field. Several modern theories started being developed at this stage. It aimed at bringing the right fit between the organization and the environment.

1930s	Systems Approach Contingency Theory	Paul Lawrence & Jay Lorsch
	Divisionalization	K. Matsushita, Alfred Sloan Jr.
	Corporate Mission	K. Matsushita, Thomas Watson
1950s	Decentralization	Peter Drucker
1960s	Organizational Structure	Alfred Chandler
1960s	Entrepreneurship	David McClelland
1970	A high reliability organization (HRO)	Karl Weick & James March
1980s	Theory Z	William Ouchi

General Management

Management innovators started looking for options to improve the overall working of the organizations. Also, as to how they create excellence.

1950s	Management by Objective	P. Drucker
1970s	Product Portfolio Management	Boston Consulting Group
	Managerial Grid	Robert Blake & Jane Mouton
1980s	S Frame work	McKinsey & co
	Excellence	Tom Peters & Robert Waterman
	Market attractiveness (3x3 cell)	General Electric

9

Corporate Strategy

It was soon realized that the difference between success and failure was in chalking out a winning strategy.

1960s	Corporate Strategy	H. Igor Ansoff
1980s	Competitive Strategy Key factors for Success	Michael Porter Kenichi Ohmae
1990s	Core Competency	C. K. Prahlad
2000s	Blue ocean strategy	Kim Chan & Renee Maubrough
	Balance Score Card	Robert Kaplan

Marketing

Marketing was discovered when demand started exceeding the supply, customer became more demanding and competition started increasing.

1950s	Customer Orientation	P. Drucker
1960s	Marketing Myopia	Theodore Levitt
1970s	Positioning	Al Ries & Jack Trout
1980s	Service Niche	Jan Carlzon
	Marketing Warfare	Al Ries & Jack Trout

1990s	Globalization of Markets	Theodore Levitt
	Political Marketing	Dilip M. Sarwate
	Serve-Qual Model	Parshuraman, Zeitmal & Berry
	Customer Delight	Japanese philosophy

Operations Management

Execution became crucial to establish a competitive advantage.

1920s	Mass Production	Henry Ford I
1930s	Quality Control	Walter Stewart
1950s	Statistical Quality Control Quality Control Systems JIT, Kanban	W. E. Deming J. M. Juran Taichi Ohmo
1980s	Quality improvements, Zero DefectsWorld Class Manufacturing	Philip Crosby R. J Schonberger

Information Management

Information was recognized as a resource. The increased volume and complexity brought in a new revolution.

1970 s	Information Age	Alvin Toffler
1980s	MIS	E. Oz
1990 s	Competitive Intelligence	Ben Gilad
	Knowledge Management WWW	Karl Sveiby Microsoft

These are some of the management innovations which have added value, increased competitiveness and are part of knowledge management.

It can be seen that the journey from 1860 to date has been very interesting. All the tools and techniques listed above are a part of management education, anywhere in the world. Some people may scoff it off as nothing but mere theory. They are mistaken. It must be realized that 'there is nothing like mere theory. The practical experiences of people have given rise to writing of these theories'. The individuals and organizations have used them. This is where the difference lies between success and the failure.

Gary Hamel was asked to identify the main innovations, which have revolutionized the management of organizations. He gave a list given below:

12 Innovations that shaped Modern Management[1]

- Scientific management (Time & motion studies)
- Cost accounting and variance analysis

- The commercial research laboratory, the industrialization of science
- ROI analysis and capital budgeting
- Large scale project management (PERT/CPM)
- Divisionalization
- Leadership development
- Industry consortia
- Radical decentralization (self-organization)
- Formalized strategic analysis.
- Employee driven problem solving (Quality circles, Kaizan)

Some of the innovations of the 21st century

- Bottom of the pyramid- Prof. Stuart Hart of Cornel University's B-School along with Prof. C.K.Prahlad of University of Michigan
- Micro finance- With Mohammed Younus of Bangladesh Gramin Vikas Bank (BGVB) winning the Nobel Prize in the year 2007
- Microcosm marketing: Relevant to SME sector, strategies on effective marketing

The pursuit of knowledge is unending. We believe that there will be many more in the years to come who will contribute towards the improvements and benefits to the stakeholders.

OOO

2 | The Culture of Innovation

Innovation has become the new buzzword for corporate chiefs. It has become the new mantra in corporate presentations and pitches to customers. However, most companies never achieve break-through innovation. They simply improve upon a product, process or service that is in existence in some form or another. Breakthrough innovation or the creation of 'killer apps' (killer application) requires a dedicated approach that relies less on luck and epiphanies and more on a culture that can encourage new ideas, refine them through a disciplined approach and place bets on the truly innovative ideas.

The innovation agenda must be drafted carefully. The captains of the company must prepare it in cognizance of the **company's culture, areas of focus, process and metrics or measures.**

Creating a culture where innovation can thrive

This area is of paramount importance if innovation has to succeed. All ideas will eventually die if a company doesn't create a culture where employees can take risks, collaborate connect, and learn from their failures. See box.

3M (Minnesota Mining & Manufacturing Company) is widely respected as a company which launches more than one hundred new products every year. The key centers on 3M's innovation- driven and supported corporate culture. 3M encourages everyone, not just its engineers, to become "product champions". Anyone who is hot about an idea is encouraged to do some homework to find out what knowledge exists, where the products could be developed in the company, whether it is patentable and how profitable it might be. If the idea finds support, a venture team is formed with volunteer representatives from R&D, Manufacturing, Marketing and Legal departments. An 'Executive Champion' who nurtures the team and protects it from bureaucratic intrusion heads each team. If a 'healthy looking' product is developed, the team stays with it and markets it. If the product fails, each team member nevertheless returns to his or her previous level. Some teams have tried three or four times to make a success of an idea, and in several cases have succeeded. Each year, 3M hands out its 'Golden Step' awards to venture teams whose new product earned more than $2 Million USA sales or $4 Million in worldwide sales within three years of its commercial introduction. Hence, more than 'Inventions', it is 'Intrapreneurship' which is the management innovation at play at 3M. More companies are seeking to use 'Intrapreneurship' in their organization. And for achieving this, it is the creation of the right culture, which is responsible for it.

Indian scenario

How many Indian companies have the appetite for taking risk? If we reflect upon the true path breaking innovations produced by Indian corporations, we realize that we have come up short in this area.

The reason is that most Indian corporations are not trained nor encouraged to take risk. The corporations that consistently rank towards the top in the list of the most innovative companies in the world have one thing in common – they encourage, even embrace risk taking. Much like the most basic concept in finance – risk and reward go hand in hand, thus, goes innovation.

Risk taking begins with a culture that gives employees the space to dream and work on ideas even if they may sound or be non-traditional or even risky. For e.g. Google offer employees one day in a week to work on their pet ideas. Services such as Google News and Google Earth have emerged from this. Recently, Hewlett Packard launched an initiative touted as Print 2.0. It invited employees to submit business ideas that could create a web based business for HP and leverage its much-vaunted printing portfolio. Such initiatives encourage employees to think creatively. By offering rewards to the contributing employees, the corporation sends a loud signal that it takes all ideas seriously.

Some corporations can take this further by allocating budget to risky ideas with good growth potential. These ideas typically start off as 'startups' within large companies – lean groups, decentralized decision making, fast track audience with senior management. Staffed with seasoned managers as well as young go-getters, it presents a mix of experience and the exuberance that is needed to help ideas succeed. It's been commonly observed that the more innovative firms have 40% or larger percentage of its revenue contributed by products that were created in the previous 3-4 years. (This scenario has been discussed above through the case on 3M)

Some truly innovative companies like Procter & Gamble have taken this concept even one step further by creating management positions such as a Vice President of Innovation whose sole responsibility is to drive innovation in all parts of the company, as well as with partners and potential customers.

Collaborate and Connect

It's key to collaborate and connect to improve the odds of producing a successful innovation.

Any innovation to succeed requires participation from different areas or functions in an organization from production, finance, marketing, HR, strategy etc. Also, within a function itself, it's important to give the idea or innovation the best 'chance' you can by collaborating with the best brains that can help the idea succeed. This may entail collaborating with people across multiple disciplines in the company, across geographies, even outside the company with partners, customers or even with competition (co-opetition). In the fast paced world of business, an idea has embarked on its course to redundancy or even irrelevance the moment it's imagined, and the only way to help an idea and an innovation succeed is to keep it fresh by constantly connecting with the best brains available.

Management should encourage collaboration by offering employees a variety of IT tools or web based tools such as wikis, share points to forums such as jams or virtual brainstorming that open submission of ideas to all parts of the companies for a fixed period of time.

IBM conducted one such jam very successfully in 2006 where for a period of 1-2 days, employees from all over the company irrespective of their heritage were encouraged to submit ideas – a virtual jam. The company has committed funds to the best ideas to emerge from this exercise.

Learning from Failures

There's a saying: 'If you lose, don't lose the lesson'. Companies that invite success by encouraging failure increase their odds of creating truly breakthrough innovations. Thomas Alva Edison, the inventor of light bulb when asked about his many failures before he successfully created the light bulb, famously remarked that through his failures he had discovered the many ways in which the light bulb couldn't be created. However, most businesses don't have the luxury of failing often even if it educates the employees on paths that don't lead them to success. Sometimes the price of failure in a business is high, so companies can mitigate the risk inherent in failure by paying extra attention to those business variables that are most likely to create a negative outcome. By doing so, they reduce the downside and greatly increase the chances of success. A popular analytical tool that supports such an analysis is the Tornado chart – the chart ranks the input variables in a business decision in descending order of magnitude i.e. those variables that produce the 'largest' swing in the result are ranked at the top. Such an analysis can help management identify the most important variables, and by taking the extra precaution to control them, the company can limit downside risk, thereby increasing its chances of success.

Areas of focus

The company should determine the areas that need most attention. This doesn't suggest that, other areas not identified as areas of focus should be neglected, because, innovation should be for one and all. It only suggests that the key focus areas will receive a larger proportion of the resources needed to make them successful. Ideas alone don't solve problems. It's the resources deployed and the actions taken to support the ideas that deliver on the promise of innovation.

The focus may consider the following options:

- Product group, which will include design, formulation, packaging and branding
- Customer group for expectations on specific attributes
- Geographical areas, which may include rural, national and international markets
- Distribution with respect to all areas of logistics.

It can also be kept in mind that this focus must give a competitive advantage to the company.

Process

The company should design processes to collect and filter ideas from all parts of the company. It's important that participation not be restricted to senior management but open to all employees.

The channels for collecting data could be simple tools such as suggestion boxes to forums designed to pitch business ideas. Companies must create tools or processes that collect ideas. Like the catchments area for a dam, a company must create a repository where ideas continue to flow in. It's the ideas that employees to a company that makes them valuable to the organization. Thus, it's important that the company makes every attempt to 'download' the brains of their employees. This is essentially achieved by thinking of the repository of ideas as a mine that can be built over time, as a source of intellectual property that can create the revenue streams of tomorrow. Such repositories, with the use of technology, can be enhanced or made intelligent enough to seek connections amongst closely related concepts or ideas and flow them to the appropriate levels in the organization.

The process should be both structured and unstructured – defined or shaped like a funnel. The base of the funnel should be broad and collect as many ideas as it can. Those ideas should be filtered on different criteria or key performance indicators. Again, this 'filter' should be driven by the key focus areas as defined by the captains of the company. Once the ideas have been filtered, they should be developed into solid business cases. The ideas should be flushed out to examine both the strategic fit with the company's goals and the customer pain point they can solve. Based on such an evaluation, the best ideas should be green-lighted for investment. It's important however to note that, holistically speaking, ideas are rarely bad, they are inappropriate either in terms of their fit with the company's charter or unfit with the times or the target customer. This again re-emphasizes the need to 'download' the brains of the employees, so that the ideas reside in the repository and can be leveraged at a suitable time.

What is a process?

- A continuous and regular action or succession of actions
- Taking place or carried on in a definite manner
- Leading to the accomplishment of some result
- A continuous operation or series of operations

Functions & processes

- Management focus has traditionally been on the functional hierarchy
- A process must cut across the functional hierarchies to meet customer expectations.

- It must encompasses all areas like R&D, Manufacturing, Marketing, Finance HRD, Logistics and others

Business Process Reengineering (BPR) is one such management innovation, which was proposed by Michael Hammer in 1990. BPR has nothing to do with engineering.

BPR has been defined as follows:

- Targeted to add value and benefits to the customers
- To achieve step improvements in performance and redesigning processes
- Can be applied at an individual process level or to the whole organization
- BPR is an improvement philosophy

Some other BPR innovations

Worldwide, there have been several management innovations which have been put under the title of BPR. Few BPR products are listed below:

- Just in time (JIT)
- Total quality management (TQM)
- Time compression management (TCM)
- Fast cycle response (FCR)
- Customer relation management (CRM)
- Kaizen
- Enterprise resource planning (ERP)
- Supply chain management (SCM)

BPR learning comes from customers, consultants, suppliers, staff,benchmarking and others. Succeeding at BPR requires drive from the top, willingness to treat people fairly and with respect, ensuring that the right sponsors are chosen and establishing clarity of purpose and design.

The message is 'communicate, communicate and communicate.

The scope of the project depends on the ambitions of the initiative, aggressive re-engineering performance targets and the context of the process being redesigned. The organization has to treat BPR as a holistic philosophy. It must aim for some quick hits and ensure that the process matches the needs of the markets it serves. It should preferably involve customers and suppliers in the redesign process. And most importantly, it must dedicate resources to the project. It must be recognized that BPR is just the beginning.

Metrics or measures

Innovation has to be nurtured as any project is - from its inception (or ideation) to its implementation. Some may deem such an approach as too restrictive, but, it's important to understand that innovation is focused on producing tangible results. These results don't have to be measured strictly in financial terms. The company that embarks on a mission of innovation can measure success in several ways. For e.g.

Innovative practices may focus on increasing customer satisfaction or lowering downtime on a production shop floor. The management of a company can decide the metrics or scorecard to measure innovation, but it's important to measure it, for as the saying goes, what gets measured gets managed. The concept may sound counter-intuitive.

One may make an argument that innovation by its very nature suggests creativity, and any creative work cannot operate within tolerances. A 'No holds barred' approach sounds appealing but it doesn't produce tangible results, because everybody is expected to embrace the mantra of innovation and nobody ever does because it's not measured and hence never managed. The company should create a scorecard that tracks 'innovation

Metrics' such as number of ideas submitted, number of proposals under development, number of new products launched, revenues from new products etc. Organizations should also consider tying part of the variable compensation of senior employees to such 'innovation' based metrics. Such alignment forces management to focus on innovation like any other key business metric.

In summary, innovation is essential and perhaps critical to the success of an organization in the modern world. Rapid advances in technology and globalization have dulled any edge a corporation may have had on productivity. In the next decade, as information technology penetrates deeply in the emerging economies, the world will become truly 'flat'.

In such a new world, only companies who can out-think and Out- innovate the competition will survive – this will require a transformation - from mere lip service to the concept of innovation to its integration into the culture and DNA of the organization.

○○○

3 | The Concept of Core Competency

The students of management were thrilled when Times of India of November 15, 2007 reported the findings of this year's Thinkers 50 rankings. For the first time in the history, an Indian - Coimbator Krishnarao (CK) Prahlad has been named the most influential management thinker alive in the world. A native of Tamil Nadu (India), he studied Physics at the University of Madras, passed out from the first batch of Indian Institute of Management, Ahmedabad and then went on to get his Ph.D. from Harvard Business School. He taught briefly in India and now is a professor Emeritus at the business school of University of Michigan, Ann Arbor, USA. What did he do to reach this hall of fame? This was on account of several of his innovative articles in Harvard Business Review, his three books, Competing for the future (1994) along with Gary Hamel, The future of Competition (2004) along with Venkat Ramaswamy and his latest The fortune at the bottom of pyramid (2006) along with Stuart Hart which has put him in this exalted position. Is he the only Indian in these top 50 rankings? There is more good news that three more thinkers of Indian origin are in this list. They are (the bracket gives their ranking),

- Professor Ram Charan (22): He is the traveling Management Guru and advisor to many organizations round the world. His several articles in Fortune, Harvard Business Review and his book Execution along with Larry Bossidy have given him this status.

- Professor Vijay Govind Rajan (23): Recently, he has joined General Electric (GE) as 'Professor in Residence' and 'Chief Innovative Consultant'.

- Professor Rakesh Khurana (45): A faculty member at Harvard Business School, his latest work looks at the development of executive education.

How is this ranking done? See below

The selection is done by the visitors to Thinkers 50 website (www.thinkers50.com) over a period of two years. As reported, the site had 84000 unique visitors, with 33,723 adding it to their favorites list. After sifting through more than 3500 votes, a list of contenders is compiled. The result is a short list of 100 names. These names are then assessed against 10 criteria. Each thinker is marked against the criteria on a scale of 1 (low) to 10 (high). The measures include the originality of idea, impact of ideas, presentation style, written communication, loyalty of followers, business sense, international outlook, rigor of research and accessibility.

The top ten in the list are given below. (The bracket gives 2005 rankings).

1. C. K. Prahlad (3)
2. Bill Gates (2)
3. Alan Greenspan (35)
4. Michael Porter (1)
5. Gary Hamel (14)

6. W. Chan Kim & Renee Mauborgne (15)

7. Tom Peters (4)

8. Jack Welch (5)

9. Richard Branson (11)

10. Jim Collins (6)

Hopefully, this list and the process through which it goes will teach a lesson to the self-styled Indian Management Guru's as to what it takes to achieve this hall of fame!

In this article, we will be discussing three management innovations, which are used worldwide. Through this, we would like to pay our tribute to Professor Prahlad, as it will include one of his innovations.

Core competency

Professor Prahlad shot to prominence with his theory of Core Competency. To put it simply, Professor Prahlad suggested that every individual and organization must identify their core strengths and should aim at consolidating the same. This can be used for chalking out their short as well as long term strategies. As it happens, every new thought is received with equal enthusiasm as well as skepticism. Prahlad had to bear with both. An illustration in the box will highlight this innovation.

- Pune's house of Kirloskar's, a 120 plus year old group is a testimony how the use of this theory resulted in this group's debacle from one of the top ten groups in the Indian industry to nowhere as of today. The mainstay of the group- Late S. L. Kirloskar always used to say that 'we are engineers first, we will grow only in engineering line'. Starting first with the manufacturing of Pumps, they went in for an

Integrative Strategy by manufacturing Diesel Engines, Electric Motors, Transformers, Machine Tools, Tractors, Castings and other engineering products. The only diversification was in hotel when they set up the first five star hotel in Pune (Hotel Blue Diamond) which they subsequently sold arguing that it does not fit in their core competency. Today, with this philosophy, the group is nowhere in the top industrial groups of India. Companies who came much later like Reliance, Bharati Televentures, Essar, Larson & Toubro, Infosys and many others have gone much ahead of them. It is sad that many group companies like Kirloskar Tractors, Mysore Kirlosksr, Shivaji Iron Works, Kirloskar Kisan and other smaller companies are no more in existence.

• A Calcutta based company, named Indian Tobacco Company was a leading manufacturer of Cigarettes in India. In 1968, the Surgeon General of USA came out with a finding that Cigarette smoking will be injurious to your health; the company realized that they would have limitations of growth if they remain in area of their core competency. A smart student of management would have advised them a growth strategy from cigarettes to Bidi, Tambaku, Gutka and other tobacco related products. The company did not pay any heed to the concept of core competency and decided to diversify in totally unrelated lines like Agriculture, Hospitality, Power Generation and many others. The name of the company was changed to ITC Ltd. This made them into one of the top groups in private sector in India today.

Does that mean that the innovation proposed by Professor Prahlad is of no merit? That is far from the truth. See this example below:

- Western India group of Industries started as distributors for Kirloskar range of products for the Eastern region in India some 50 years back. This they did to the best of their abilities for almost 40 years or more. When the third generation came in the business, he was not very happy with a mere turnover of Rs. 50 millions in this period. He had great ambitions to take the group to Rs.50, 000 million by the turn of the century. He diversified in some 34 areas which included making energy from solid waste, dry docks, manufacturing of sugar, oil refinery in Dubai, financial services, travel services and many more. None of them had any relationship to their core business. The company came out with a public issue of Rs.1600 million which was over subscribed. With poor management, the group collapsed with accumulated liabilities of over Rs.4000 millions. Today the group is dead, the chairman absconding and all stakeholders are losers. A good example of growth strategies, which ignored the concept of core competency.

This also brings to notice that the Thinkers come out with their innovations based on their own experiences. It is for the user to apply it correctly depending on the situation. It may be applicable correctly in some situations while it may not in another. That does not belittle the value of the innovation.

Competitive advantage of nations

Professor Michael Porter is another great thinker particularly in areas of Strategy where he came out with his innovations. Undoubtedly, that makes him one of the greatest advisors in this area. Some 20 years back, he came out with his book Competitive Advantage of Nations. What makes a country, region and/or an organization great? Porter provides the answer with his model in this book.

Porter talks about his model under six headings. They are:

1. Factor conditions: This would include the manufacturing capacities available, quality of labor, availability or otherwise of infrastructure and similar aspects.

2. Demand conditions: This will evaluate the size of the market, growth rate over last few years, potential for future and other aspects. This will not only look into the domestic market but also the global market that can be reached.

3. Related and supporting industries: This will also cover a wide range of services needed which will include financial services, insurance, transportation, warehousing, testing, inspection, advertising and many others. What has become important today is the presence of global services in this area, which can generate more confidence with foreign buyers.

4. Firm strategy, structure and rivalry: To enhance once own competitiveness, Strategy will be king. A dynamic strategy will have to be chalked. This will also require effective organizational development, investment in good people and continuous learning. An environment that has competitive forces will ensure striving for excellence.

5. Chance: only those will succeed who will dare to take on challenges. It cannot be left to chance. Taking risk to build a competitive advantage becomes essential.

6. Government: Whether you like it or not, the government does play a major role. It can come out with policies, incentives and many other fiscal benefits, which can

prove beneficial to an organization. Remember, the Japanese government for several years gave a cash subsidy to Japanese companies as high as 50% whereby they could make a big impact in global markets for automobiles, entertainment electronic items, calculators, watches, cameras and many other products.

Porter was invited by Confederation of Indian Industries (CII) to identify the sectors from Indian economies, which give them a competitive advantage. He listed 22 sectors in 1989 which are given below:

- Agriculture produce
- Agricultural implements
- Auto components
- Bicycles
- Chemicals
- Crockery
- Drugs & pharmaceuticals
- Entertainment products (music, films)
- Gems & Jewelry
- Granite
- Handicrafts
- Processed food
- Leather products
- Low cost housing
- Marine food
- Metal products (castings & forgings)
- Small business
- Spices

- Textiles including readymade garments
- Tourism

Mind well, this list was prepared when India was not discovered as a favored destination for IT and ITES sectors. Today, this list requires modifications as the environmental conditions have changed drastically. However, Porter's model provides a basis for starting the thinking process.

SWOT analysis

This is one of the most commonly used tools by the students of B-Schools in Case Analysis. However, whether it is used exhaustively or not needs to be verified. What does it do?

Environmental scanning

The tool begins with identifying opportunities as well as threats (O&T) which are posed by the environment on the organization, its products/services and people. But for any purposeful action on the part of the management, the organization could be threatened with losses or may miss the opportunities. The scanning will have to be done under the following heads:

- **Economy:** This will include such factors like rainfall, GDP growth & decline, balance of payment, FDI flows, value of Indian currency, rate of inflation, recession or boom in specific sectors and many others. A continuous tracking of changes taking place can guide the management to take appropriate actions.

- **Technology:** This will include issues like technological obsolescence, increasing cost of R&D, product and/ or process developments, collective R&D and many others. It should not be forgotten what Theodore

Levitt said in his pioneering article Marketing Myopia in the sixties that 'If your own R&D does not make your product obsolete, someone else's would'.

- **Public policy:** The type of governance, their policies would have a major impact on decision making. Take for instance, how with the resistance from Left Parties in India, the policy of Privatization has been put on back burner. The other issues like Indo-US Nuclear Deal, FDI in certain sectors are also being debated.

- **Culture:** The changes taking place on account of Culture will impact several sectors of our economy. They include entertainment, food processing, textiles, readymade garments, higher education and many others. They cannot be ignored.

It will be seen that each of these aspects of macro-economy will have different impact on different industries. Economy can affect all types of industries but it will have more impact on agriculture, engineering and may be housing. Technology will affect IT, pharmaceuticals and few such industries. Public policy will have impact on all industries. The culture mostly will have impact on FMCG industries, entertainment, clothing & fashion.

Internal analysis

This will evaluate the strengths & weaknesses (S&W) which an organization possesses or lacks it. It will have to be studied under the following heads:

R&D: Whether the organization possesses the talents for R&D and whether it has the necessary budgets for the same. Alternatively, whether it can procure the desired technology to enhance its competitiveness.

Manufacturing: Whether the organization has the installed capacity, which can give it the competitive advantage in terms of economies of scale, location of plants, quality assurance, productivity and such details under this heading.

Marketing: Whether the company has adequate product differentiation, competitive pricing, distribution network, brand equity, an aggressive sale force and so on.

Human resources: This again will have to be evaluated in terms of both quantity and quality, a motivated staff, low attrition rate and many other aspects.

Leadership: This is the most crucial thing, which can really give a competitive advantage to an organization. An enlightened leader, visionary, motivator can take the organization to greater heights and vice versa.

The box gives an illustration to demonstrate the use of SWOT analysis.

We are taking an example of Infosys Technology Ltd. to demonstrate the use of SWOT analysis.

Threats: Dependence on American markets, the slowdown of American economy, weakening of US dollar, China and other third world countries emerging as destinations for outsourcing in IT area, technological obsolescence, high rate attrition of staff.

Opportunities: Emergence of markets other than USA, more industrial sectors going for computerization, IT consultancy, rising demand ITES, development of IT products, earnings in foreign currency thereby reduction in tax liability and many others.

Weaknesses: Limitations of growth in Bangalore due to bottlenecks in infrastructure.

Strengths: High quality of leadership, succession planning in order, conducive work culture, excellent brand equity, creation of wealth for all stakeholders, high level of ethics, corporate social responsibility and many others.

This analysis will help the organization in chalking out the growth strategies. This may include opening offices in India and abroad to effect cost control, proximity to markets, identifying new areas to enter and many others.

It can be seen from the above, how the management innovations can be put to use. This can be done for a nation, a region as well as for an organization. India has to compete with at least 40 developed and developing countries in the world. The major threat coming from China. Using these three tools, the analysis can lead to overcome the weaknesses and putting the strengths to use. Individuals to evaluate the competitiveness can also use these tools. The real success is in its use and drawing conclusions, which can be used for formulating the strategy.

OOO

4 | Tools for Strategic Planning

One author aptly captured the need for **strategic planning** by saying that; we should all be concerned about the future, because, that is where we are going to spend the rest of our lives'.

Indians, in general, do not have much faith in Planning. They would rather leave everything to destiny. Is it right? This statement may shock you, but in our survey of some leading industrialists, planning, as an inherent part of a company's strategy, was de-emphasized for a variety of reasons. Here are some sound bites:

- I do not know whether I will be surviving after one year or not.

- Yes, of course I have my future plans ready in my mind. They are all confidential.

- No, I have neither documented them nor shared them with my colleagues. In any case, they are too dumb to understand.

- The markets are changing so rapidly; no purpose will be served by doing any planning.

We believe that there is no substitute to Planning. It's simple: How can you be prepared for the future without preparing for it? A good plan prepares for the future by defining the planning period, the tools & techniques to craft the plan and the modus operandi to execute it, be it through a centralized or a decentralized structure. Here's a formal definition of 'planning'.

Def. Planning: (noun) It is ideally a search in the future, to situate the company in the present, to take care of all environmental threats & opportunities.

There are at least 22 definitions we can offer on Planning. However, it is more important to understand the Process of planning. It seeks answers to following questions:

1. Where does the company stand as on say December 31, 2015? Understanding some key metrics such as could expand the answer to this question: sales turnover, profitability, market share, productivity and many others.

2. How has the company reached this position say in last five years? A trend analysis of key metrics such as market share, revenue etc. can provide insight into the primary drivers of growth or decline (as the case may be).

3. Where will the company be in say 5 years? This will help us define the vision, mission, goals and targets for the company.

4. How will the company get there? This will define the strategy, policies and a time bound action plan.

In this article, we will be discussing two management innovations, which are used for strategic planning. These tools provide answers to first two questions as given in the planning process.

Product Portfolio Management (BCG Matrix)

The Boston Consulting Group (BCG), a leading management consulting firm, developed and popularized the growth-share matrix as shown in the figure.

The vertical axis indicates the annual growth rate of the market in which the business operates. It can range from 0 percent to 50 percent or more. A market growth rate over 20 percent can be considered as high. The horizontal axis refers to the relative market share vis-a-vis the major competitors in this market. Notice the units given on the horizontal axis thus dividing the relative market share into high and low share.

BCG PRODUCT PORTFOLIO MATRIX

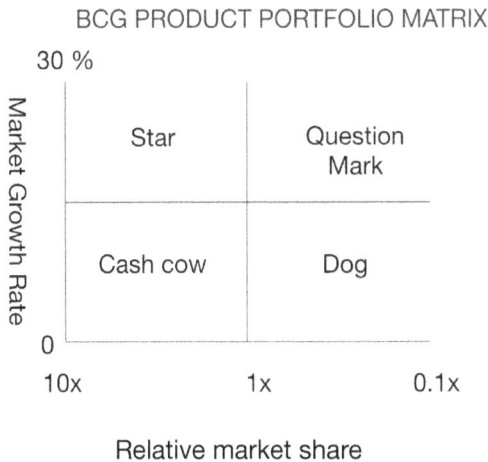

Relative market share

Dilip M. Sarwate

The growth-share matrix is divided into four cells indicating the position of company's products in these markets. They are,

Stars: This is a product where the company is enjoying a high market share as well as high growth. This is typically true of new product launched which meets with

37

favor from the customers. The company becomes the market leader. This does not mean that the company is registering a positive cash flow and profits at this stage. The company has to still overcome the R & D and market development costs. The company must spend substantially to keep up with the high market growth and to ward off the competition. A company may have more than one star.

Cash cow: This comprises of products where the market growth rate has started falling but the company still enjoys a large market share. As most of the costs have been written off, this product generates lot of cash and higher profit margins. The company is the market leader and is enjoying economies of scale.

Question marks: Products, with low market share in high growth markets are called 'question marks'. The sales over a period show erratic pattern of highs and lows. 'Question mark' products generate several questions for the company:

- Should the company discontinue the product?

   - Should they pump more money in marketing efforts?

   - Should   they modify the product?

And many more such questions. Some authors have also given the name for these products as problem children, which also looks very appropriate.

Dog products: These are the products where the company finds a declining market growth as well as low market share. This could be because of technological obsolescence and/or changing tastes of customers. The best option for the company is to discontinue this line.

The following illustrates how this management tool can be put to use.

Maruti Suzuki Ltd. came in the market in 1983 with its Maruti 800 model priced at only Rs.52, 000/-. For the first time, the Indian customer got a taste of the latest technology in four wheelers. Soon, it out surpassed the two existing manufacturers, namely, Premier Automobiles and Hindustan Motors. It remained a market leader with over 70 percent market share till 1987. The liberalization in 1991 saw many car companies entering the four-wheeler market in India. The company expanded their product line, and today, it has 24 models in its stable. Even today, it is the market leader with little over 50 percent market share. How are their different models faring? Can the BCG product portfolio matrix be used to evaluate the performance of their various models? The answer is in affirmative.

Presently, their Swift and SX4 models are termed as Star products with a waiting period, higher prices in comparison to the same class of automobiles. However, Maruti 800 is undoubtedly their Cash cow. It is still the most popular car with a high market share on account of its price and fuel efficiency. Maruti Van is a Question mark. Maruti Omni model can be considered as a Dog product.

b.   The general insurance companies (GIC) in India offer close to 170 products. It will be unwise to expect that all of them perform equally well. The Pareto concept of 80:20 is applicable. This means that 80 percent of the business comes from 20 percent of the products in the company's portfolio. They may include Vehicle insurance, Medi-claim as some of the more popular products as compared to Loss of profit, Policy for the unborn child as few others, which could not take off. The GI companies will have to find out which of their products can be classified as Star, Cash cow, Question marks and Dog products.

The practical utility of the BCG Matrix

The student and practicing managers will have to learn how to use this or any other management tool for any organization. Their skills will be tested in its application. Here are few of the tips on its utility:

- This tool can be put to use only for companies who can be described as multi-product multi-market companies. It cannot be used by a company, which has only a single product and is operating only in a local market.

- In order to use it, you require data on the total market consumption, company sales and its relative market share at least for last five years or so to observe any trends.

- Having classified the product mix in these four categories, the management can take a decision on strategy for each of the products. These are called as Strategic Business Units (SBU's). They can be treated as independent profit centers, have their own set of competitors and a different strategy can be developed for each.

- The categorization can keep on changing with respect to changing market environments.

Mc Kinsey 7-S Frame work

Tom Peters and Robert Waterman Jr. wrote their best seller In Search of excellence: Lessons from America's Best Run Companies in 1982. This was the first study of its kind, which gave rise to a spate of similar studies to identify Excellent companies. They were then working with McKinsey & Company, undoubtedly the world's leading strategic management consulting firm. This was the model they offered in this book. The consultants believe that Strategy is only one of seven elements in successful business practice. The figure below shows this model.

The first three elements – strategy, structure and systems are considered the 'hardware' of success. The next four-style, skills, staff and shared values- are   the 'software'. What do they mean? How can this tool be used for organizational success?

Strategy: These are the decision variables to achieve the organizational objectives. These include various options the company can pursue for a short as well as on long-term basis.

Structure: This studies whether the company has well defined organization structure with its hierarchy, channels of communication, authorities and accountability.

Systems: This studies whether the company has well defined systems and procedures for all the operations. They could be from material procurement to order execution.

Style: This studies the leadership style from autocratic to democratic, work culture, productivity and whether the employees share a common way of thinking and behaving. This may include customer care and customer satisfaction.

Skills: This aims at ascertaining whether the employees have the skills needed to fulfill the aims and objectives of the organization.

Staffing: This studies whether the company has hired the right kind of people both quantitatively as well as qualitatively, trained them well, assigned them the right jobs.

Shared values: This aims at finding out whether the employees share the same passion and guiding principles. When these elements are present, companies have been found to be more successful in achieving their objectives.

7 - S FRAMEWORK BY McKINSEY & CO.

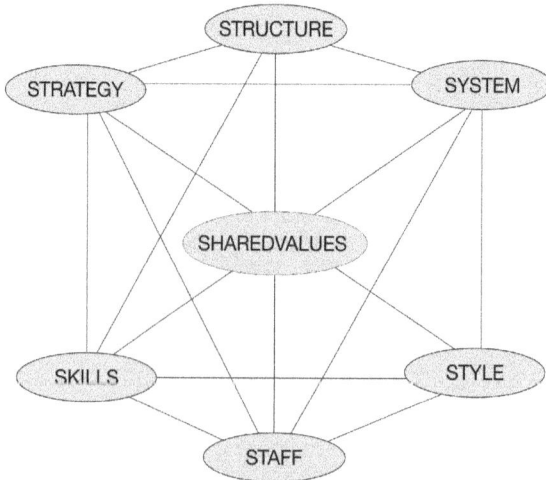

Dilip M. Sarwate

This model assesses the internal environment, its strengths & weaknesses under these heads. Then it can be used to recommend strategies aiming mainly at cultural transformation of the organization for success. McKinsey & Company, which has a strong presence in India, has used this model for number of companies, both in public and private sectors. The box gives an illustration how it can be used.

Indian Posts & Telegraph department (P & T) undoubtedly is a government organization which is wide spread and employs a large number of people. Since independence it has provided yeomen service to the entire nation. Over the years, it has faced competition from private courier services. The advent of technology in the form of e-mail has reduced its need at least for urban India. What are the choices available for them to plan their future? How can this model be used for them? We offer our suggestions:

Strategy: We have no knowledge whether the P & T Department has prepared a long term plan, whether their strategies are in place, new products they plan to launch, old one which they want to discontinue as they have outlived their lives, strategic alliances they are planning and so on., There is room for doubt that perhaps, this is missing. May be a rough plan might be available but the finer details are missing.

Structure: The organization structure is very well in place. However, the duties & responsibilities are clearly undefined. Many times we experience lack of service because the person who is handling a certain function is on leave. The contingency measures are certainly missing making customers complaining bitterly.

Systems: The above example clearly demonstrates that what is needed is mainly the systems correction. Even in the era of Globalization, the organization is perceived as a typical government organization with its lethargy and incompetence.

Style: The style is mostly beauracratic. Red tape is very much common. No one will have a second opinion that it needs radical change.

Skills: The skills required to make the organization techno-savvy are nonexistent.

Staff: The morale of the staff is at low level. Remuneration is not keeping in tune with the changing times. This results in not attracting talented persons to the organization.

The present staff is hard working and honest but lacks professionalism.

Shared values: We have not noticed any vision, which can be inspiring to the staff. It badly needs a vision which will be shared by all and motivate them for a paradigm change.

This analysis will lead to developing a strategy under different headings, which will have to fulfill the SMART Formula namely, specific, measurable, attainable, relevant and time bound.

The discerning readers, through these illustrations, will understand the tools and their utility. The analysis by itself does not provide solutions. It only tells the organization where it is. It can only provide the road maps. However, where to go will have to be decided by the CEO. This is his inescapable responsibility, which he cannot delegate. For, 'if he does not know where he is going, any road will take him there'.

The Auto Expo 2008 in New Delhi created a history sort of. On January 10, Tata's brought on display, amidst lights and fanfare, their 624 cc, four seater passenger car named Nano. Priced at USD 2500 or Rupees One Lakh at the dealer end, the car is the cheapest four-wheeler in the world. It is a testimony to India's designing and frugal manufacturing skills. The project was initiated when Mr. Ratan Tata- Chairman of the company saw a middle class family of four riding on a two-wheeler on a rainy day in Mumbai. He felt sorry for them for the risks they were undertaking and decided to develop a four-wheeler, which they can afford. It promises to herald the second road revolution in India since the launch of the Maruti 800 in 1983.

The following gives the specifications for the Tato Nano:

Engine: 624 cc, 33 bhp   Fuel efficiency: Over 20 kmpl

Safety: Meets international norms   Emission: Euro 4 compliant

Gear box: 4-speed, manual   Fuel tank: 30 litre

Other features: Front disc brakes and drums in the rear

Top speed: 90 kmph   Space: 21 per cent more than Maruti 800

Price: Rs. 1 lakh excluding taxes and transportation cost. On road. price is estimated to be Rs.1.25 lakh

Discussions have already started whether Tata's will meet with success with this product or not? Will the Indian consumers accept the product? They are estimated to create a capacity of producing around 300,000 Nano's per year. The skeptics are already shouting about traffic jams on the roads.

And you don't have to be a marketing wizard to figure out its potential. Growing at 9 per cent, India's GDP is over a trillion dollars (Rs. 40 lakh crores) delivering an average per capita income of USD 1000 (Rs.40,000). Currently, 80 lakh two-wheelers, 13 lakh four-wheelers and 3 lakh three-wheelers are sold in India every year. Add to this, 5 lakh used car sales. Hypothetically, each of these buyer is a potential customer of Nano. The launch of Nano is timed to perfection and it is bound to click.

Did Tata's study any management model before launching Nano? We have no knowledge about it. However, we feel that two models, which we are going to discuss in this article, will be most appropriate to study the launch of Nano and developing a strategy for the same. This also will show how management innovations help take business decisions? Once again, the knowledge is available. The effective utilization will bring the results.

GE Market attractiveness Model

Jack Welch, the legendary CEO of General Electric (GE) took over the company when the turnover was close to 8 billion USD. When he retired, he had left with an impressive turnover of close to 300 billion USD. How did he achieve it? Jack was very clear in his mind. He decided his strategy by spelling out to quit businesses where GE was not either number one or two. He used a model shown graphically below which is described as GE Market Attractiveness Model.

MARKET ATTRACTIVENESS

STRONG	MEDIUM	WEAK	
PROTECT POSITION	INVEST TO BUILD	BUILD SELECTIVEL	High
BUILD SELECTIVELY	MANAGE FOR EARNING	LIMITED EXPANSION	Medium
PROTECT & REFOCUS	MANGE FOR EARNINGS	DIVEST OR CLOSE	Low

BUSINESS STRENGTHS

MARKET ATTRACTIVENESS

On the X-axis, it gives the strengths of the business organization under the headings of Strong, Medium and Weak and on the Y-axis the market attractiveness under the headings of High, Medium and Low.

The **Business strengths** are identified under the following heads:

a) R & D capabilities

b) Economies of scale and unit costs

c) Product quality

d) Market share

e) Brand equity

f) Distribution network

g) Promotional effectiveness

h) Managerial competence

The **Market attractiveness** is identified under the following heads:

- Overall market size and growth rate
- Competitive intensity
- Historical profit margin
- Technological requirements
- Environmental impact
- Consumer acceptability

The GE matrix is divided into nine cells. That is why; many times it is called a 3x3 matrix. The box gives its relevance to launch of Nano.

The GE model evaluates the market attractiveness with the business strengths. This exercise leading to formulation of strategies.

Market attractiveness

Let us study some of the salient features of the Indian market for passenger cars.

- Out of the 23 lakh passenger cars made in the country, almost 70 percent are in the small category. The popular models being Maruti 800, Zen, Alto, Santro and others. As such, the demand for smaller cars is more.

- Out of 80 lakh two-wheelers consumed, with the rise in the family size, the upper 20 percent families would like to go for a four-wheeler. However, the gap between the average two-wheeler price of Rs.40, 000/ and the cheapest four-wheeler at say Rs.200, 000/, the gap was quite wide. The affordability was also an issue. Hence, if a product was made available at around Rs.100, 000/ in four-wheelers, the acceptability was assured.

- Presently, Tata Motors are Market Followers behind Maruti Suzuki and Hyundai. Hence, Tata's will have to look for a segment in the market, which they can capture. As of now, no four-wheeler in that price range is available in the market.

- Tata's identified a niche segment, which will prove most attractive for them in the Indian markets.

Organizational strengths

- Tata Motors is in manufacturing of four wheelers now for over 40 years. They entered in the passenger car market some 20 years back but met with failure initially with their Sierra and Estate models. Even, the SUV Safari has a very small market in India due to its large size, high fuel consumption and narrow Indian roads. Tata's came in a big way in passenger car market with launch of Indica first and Indigo later. But, they remained a distant third behind Maruti and Hyundai.

- The organization has large number of design experts, skilled manpower to come out with new models.

- The proposed factory to manufacture Nano at Singur in West Bengal met with political resistance. At the time of writing this article, the Kolkata High Court has granted them permission to acquire land and start manufacturing operations. The West Bengal Government has offered them several benefits to start their factory, which will enable them to make Nano at a low price.

- With the earlier two models, the distribution structure is in place. The before and after sales services are assured.

- The most important strength of Tata's is their Brand Equity. This will be helping them the most in marketing of Nano.

Porter's model on competitive forces

Professor Michael Porter undoubtedly is one of the leading strategists in the world today. His model given below on evaluating the competitive forces in launching a product is very helpful to start-ups as well as running companies.

PORTER'S MODEL ON COMPETITIVE FORCES

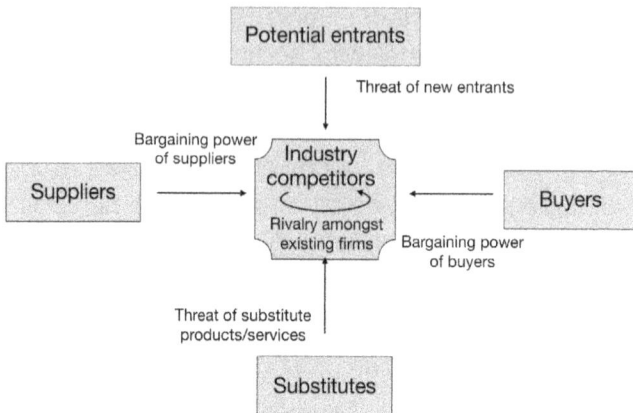

Dilip M. Sarwate

He recommends five forces, which need to be evaluated properly to come out with business decisions. They include the following:

- Industry competition-rivalry amongst firms: This studies the present competitive scenario in the market. The competition can be looked coming from Brand (similar product, for example a motor-cycle), Form (similar products but available in different forms like motor-cycle, scooter and a moped), Industry (two-wheelers, three-wheelers and four wheelers) and finally Generic competition (automobiles, railways and airlines). The share of each competing products then can be evaluated.

- Buyers: It studies the bargaining powers of the buyers and the willingness to pay a certain price for the attributes offered.

- Substitutes: It evaluates the threats that can be posed from the substitute products. In recent times, the Volvo buses running between Mumbai and Pune have taken over the business from Railways. Similarly, the Low Cost Carriers (LCC) are posing a threat again to Railways.

- Suppliers: In order to develop competitive products, the suppliers of raw materials and components also will require proper study. The Japanese brought lighter and more fuel-efficient cars in the market using engineering plastics thereby posing a big threat to American and European cars using more of metals.

- Potential entrants: In the era of globalization and competition, a new product inadvertently attracts potential entrants in the market. The company's, who come out with innovations, find that in a very short time, imitators enter the market. The latter starts with the advantage of low R & D cost, low lead-time, less marketing efforts, less risks and early profitability.

As can be seen from the above, this model can help in evaluating the competition and take decisions accordingly. The box gives two illustrations to explain the use of this model.

---

1. The case of Child Restraints

The authors' carried out an interesting consultancy assignment for an Australian company recently. The company is a leader in manufacturing 'Child Restraints'. The UNO has requested all the countries in the world to make it compulsory to use Child Restraint in the age group of 1 day to 8 years. The name did not make any sense to us, at least initially. The commercial name is simply 'Baby Car seats'. The Australian company armed with statistics in India felt that the market was ripe enough to accept the product. Every year close to 20 million

---

babies are born. Last year, 13-lakh passenger cars were sold in India, the per capita income with IT boom now is touching close to USD1000 (Rs.40, 000). However, they were wise enough to call for a feasibility study to work out the options available. The market research was done in Bangalore, Pune and Mumbai. While studying the feasibility, we used the Porters Model on Competitive Forces as discussed below:

Industry competitors- rivalry among existing firms: At the time of study, we felt that this did not exist. As such, the market looked virgin, a Blue Ocean!

Buyers: The potential buyers could be in any demography. But, they were mostly urban, upper middle-income group, with higher education and those who have visited and stayed in other developed countries of the world. This description fitted IT professionals the best. The number of IT professionals is on the rise. At an average price of Rs.5000/ per seat, the affordability was not a problem. One who can afford to buy a minimum Rs. 200,000/ worth of car, for the love and safety of his/her child, can easily afford this product. As such, prima facie the market looked very attractive.

Substitutes: The major substitute was, of course, the lap of the mother. The rich could afford to have a maid for the same purpose. It was not that the market had not heard of Baby Car seats. There were imported car seats coming from Italy, USA and China ranging in prices from Rs.2000/ to Rs. 9000/ per seat. A local manufacturer was making a crude version and selling some 3000 pieces in a year priced at around Rs.2500/.

Suppliers: The raw materials and components were not that critical, which could have posed any problems.

Potential entrants: There was every likelihood that competition would emerge if they come to know of the great potential. Actually, one company, a joint venture with an Automobile major from India and a US company, which supplied seats for the former was actually making the car seats in the US markets. We could not solicit from them their lack of interest to enter this product line.

We had to come out with market estimation and strategies on promotion and distribution. The issue also involved deciding whether to begin with import of the products in fully finished form or in 'Semi Knocked Down' (SKD) form or to set up a full scale manufacturing operation.

2. The case of Tata Nano

This model can be used for Tata Nano very effectively.

- Industry competition: The data on Indian automobile industry comprising mainly of four-wheelers, three wheelers and two-wheelers is available exhaustively. Amongst passenger cars, the share of Small. Medium, Executive and Premium cars is also known accurately. The trends over the years also are available.

- Buyers: 80 per cent buyers for passenger cars are individuals or families. They can be broken down demographically to know their shares. Nano will be targeted to middle income consumers, mostly the first time buyers of passenger cars.

- Substitute products; there are number of substitute products available to meet the transportation needs. However, the immediate competition coming from the two-wheelers.

- Suppliers: The cost analysts are wondering how Tata's can launch a four-wheeler at this price. The success also lies in their bargaining power with suppliers.

The attractive volumes will make the components cheaper thereby making the car at low price.

- Potential entrants: The media is already abuzz with the news on several potential entrants in small cars. The main ones include Bajaj, Ford and Honda?

This type of evaluation can give a direction to Tata's to chalk out their competitive strategies.

It must not be forgotten that to use any model, we require substantial data. This should be at least for last 4-5 years (past), the present and the future for next 4-5 years. The data when processed will become information and knowledge respectively. It should not be forgotten that it is not the information, which helps in taking decisions. The decisions are made on options. That is the key to success in strategy formulation.

OOO

5 | Generic Growth Strategies

What comes first? Theory or practice? Did the management thinkers develop the innovations first or were they conceived after a careful review of the practices that produced results? These questions have baffled students and practitioners in management. In this article, we want to address this topic. See box.

Illustration 1: Pune based Venkateshwara Hatcheries Limited undoubtedly is the leaders in Poultry industry in India. How did it reach this position? As the story goes, the founder Dr. B. V. Rao started his career as an employee at a poultry farm. Within a short time, he understood the intricacies of business. The entrepreneurial aspirations also came to the fore. He set up his first poultry firm with 'Egg Layers'. This was soon followed with another poultry farm for 'Meat Layers'. He soon found out that he had to depend on a hatchery to get his raw materials- one day old commercial birds. This is when he decided to set up his own hatchery under the present name. This also required investing in the grand parent stocks which he got of the American origin- 'Babcock'. This move was followed by a series of growth strategies to make the company offer everything under one roof in the area of Poultry. This included setting up of a 'Feed mill' - an important ingredient to get eggs or meat.

Some 35 years back, the poultry used to get affected by diseases which could wipe out the entire flock putting the farmers at great financial risk. To overcome this problem, he started Ventri Pharma offering vaccines for birds. A study of American markets showed that customers preferred 'prime cuts' – drumsticks and chicken breasts rather than the whole broiler. He started offering these and thereby started commanding a higher price. A Broiler plant followed. The era of the American Fast food was yet to dawn in the Indian markets. Sensing an opportunity, he started two fast food outlets in Pune which offered a variety of chicken dishes. He discovered that consumption of eggs dropped during the summer months. The surplus eggs produced by his hatcheries presented a problem and an opportunity. The problem – Prices declined by as much as 50%, the opportunity – surplus eggs. He was lucky that Central food & Technological Research Institute (CFTRI) had developed a technology to convert raw eggs into egg powder using spray drying technology. Using this technology, he launched the next project called Balaji Foods Ltd. in Hyderabad to manufacture Egg Powder. This product had excellent export potential and the plant prospered winning many awards. Looking at the demand of the consumers for 'ready to eat products', the company presently offers a variety of popular chicken dishes like Butter Chicken, Chicken Kheema and others. Besides the ones quoted above, the company may have come out with many other growth strategies over the years.

The question is whether they referred to any management text book giving the alternative strategies and went about them in systematic manner? Or they came out with strategies first, which later on management thinkers put them in the form of management innovations?

Illustration 2: The first joint stock company in the Kirloskar group is Kirlsokar Brothers Limited (KBL) which was set up some time around 1920's at Kirloskarwadi to manufacture pumps. The founder of Kirloskar group, late Shri Laxmanrao Kirloskar wanted to develop products which would be beneficial to the Indian farmers. Starting first with Mechanical ploughs, later they started manufacturing Pumps. He soon realized that he required a prime mover to run a pump. Thus, the second factory to manufacture Diesel Engines came up in Pune under the name of Kirloskar Oil Engines Ltd.(KOEL). This was followed by Kirloskar Electric Ltd. (KEC) coming up in Bangalore to manufacture Electrical Motors. As these were engineering products, machine tools were needed. Hence, the next factory to manufacture the same came up at Harihar under the name of Mysore Kirloskar Ltd. (MKL). All engineering products required castings and hence Shivaji Iron Works came up at Solapur. With Diesel Engines as major component, a plan came up to manufacture Road rollers and Tractors respectively. Kirloskar group once upon a time had close to 28 independent organizations. Barring perhaps the exception of Hotel Blue Diamond, all of them were closely 'Integrated' to one another. This also followed the philosophy of Late Shri S. L. Kirloskar that "we would like to grow only in Engineering line which we understand and have a core competency in".

Do you see any pattern in the strategies used by these two organizations? It is very much there which has given rise to management innovation which can be used by almost any and every organization.

Generic Growth Strategies

An organization can be categorized under the following heads:

- A start up
- A running organization struggling for survival
- A running organization doing reasonably well but nothing extra-ordinary
- A running organization doing very well
- A company which is loss making and requires turn around management

An organization could be in SME or Large sector, may belong to public, private or other sectors, and may be in manufacturing, trading, services and other sectors.

Same strategies cannot be put to use for each of these organizations. We have to find that a model is available which can be put to use for all types of organizations listed above.

Three alternatives are available. The first is to identify the opportunities to achieve further growth within current businesses (Intensive growth opportunities). The second is to build or acquire businesses that are related to current businesses (Integrative growth opportunities). The third is to identify opportunities to add attractive businesses that are unrelated to current businesses (Diversification growth opportunities).

Intensive Growth strategies

The first and foremost course of any organization is to review whether any opportunity exists for improving its existing business performance. This envisages that no new investments will be made and no new products/

services would be developed. Ansoff proposed a useful framework for detecting new intensive growth opportunities called a 'product market expansion grid' as given on the next page. This model will be of particular use for organizations which are struggling and will find it difficult to make any new investments. The alternatives discussed below will make this model clear.

a. Market penetration strategy: This will further give rise to three alternative strategies. We will take an illustration of 'Toothpastes' to illustrate the point. They are:

- Increasing consumption: The toothpaste manufacturers try to educate the customers to increase their consumption. If the customers have been brushing their teeth once every day, the manufacturer would like to convince about the benefits of brushing the teeth, twice or even thrice for better dental care.

- Winning over the competitor's customers: Undoubtedly, in every sphere, competition is on the rise. The toothpaste market is no exception. Every manufacturer, therefore, would like to win over the competitors customers through product differentiation, offering incentives and using brand ambassadors to achieve these objectives.

- Converting the non-users into users: It is strange that in India, less than 20 percent population uses toothpaste. That does not mean that the remaining are unhygienic and are not bothered about their dental care. That means, that a majority of population is using alternatives in the form of tooth powder or 'Datauan', a branch of Neem tree which is still popularly used by the village population. The statistics can convince that a great potential for toothpastes is yet to be tapped in India.

b. Market development strategy: An organization must look for new markets continuously. The markets would be of two types namely,

- New geographical markets: A successful business must grow from local to regional, to national and finally to international markets. This strategy can increase the volumes multifold.

- New end users: There will be many users who can use the existing products and/or processes. A re-look at market segmentation will help in identifying new usages.

c. New product development: This does not mean investments in 'Innovations' Rather, this aims at modifying the existing products to suit the market requirements. This may include improving the aesthetics of the product, improved packaging, improved efficiency and others. The trends in different industries are obvious. The electronic industries are going for miniaturization. Take for example industries like computers, entertainment where this is aptly applicable. While for the core engineering sectors, the trends are towards maximization of capacities. This is on account of Globalization where increased capacities will result in economies of scale and increased competitiveness.

It must not be forgotten that retaining the existing customers is cheaper than trying to woo the competitor's customers or converting the non-users into users. The last two would require considerable marketing efforts resulting in increased spending on marketing! Box gives a practical example where this model was put to use by the authors in a consultancy assignment.

An ancillary industry was manufacturing two products namely, fuel tanks and silencers for a four wheeler and a two wheeler manufacturer respectively. When the boom period prevailed, the unit operated at 100 per cent capacity utilization. However, recession struck the automobile industry and their order booking came down to 50 per cent.

In desperation, they approached the authors for guidance. In less than 15 minutes using the Ansoff model, the consultants gave them advice which in a short duration brought the ancillary unit back to full utilization of capacity. How was this achieved?

Existing products new customers: The unit was dependant only on two OEM's. They had not made any efforts to develop new customers over the years as their capacity utilization was full.

The Consultants recommended that they should make efforts to generate business from other two and four wheeler manufacturers in the country. As they were already supplying to two of the largest manufacturers, penetration was not difficult.

• New products existing customers: The unit had not made any efforts to develop new products for the existing customers. It was found that many OEM's were reducing the number of their vendors. As such, this was a good opportunity to develop new products for the existing customers with the available facilities. The relationship which was there for over 25 years would have surely ensured them to develop new products.

• New product new segments: The unit prided itself in manufacturing fuel tanks and silencers for number of years for two auto giants in the country. They did not realize that their core competency lay not in making products but in the process which they employed. The latter was 'manufacturing press components'. They were asked to explore the markets for 'Press Components' for other than Auto Sector. The proximate customers included manufacturers of washing machines, refrigerators and many other white goods which needed 'press components'. A visit to them, bringing their purchase executives to see the facilities resulted in getting orders from totally new segments.

- Export markets: The Company had never thought of offering their products for overseas buyers. India is undoubtedly emerging as a preferred destination for Auto Components. This strategy would have taken a longer time to fructify but was worth exploring.

- Entering spare components markets: The automobile companies get the spares manufactured from their vendors, put their stamp of quality control and then mark up the prices. The so called genuine spares are always priced higher. No wonder that close to 80 percent of this market is dominated by the grey suppliers. Hence, it was decided to enter in this market with quality spares. However, this could have resulted in a clash with the OE Customer. It was then decided that a separate company will manufacture the components and market them as spares under a different brand name.

All these strategies resulted in the unit operating again at 100 per cent capacity within three months. Hats off to the use of Ansoff model in revitalizing an ailing organization!

The model is given on next page.

Products

	Present	New
Present	Market Penetration	Product Development
New	Market Development	Diversification

(Markets)

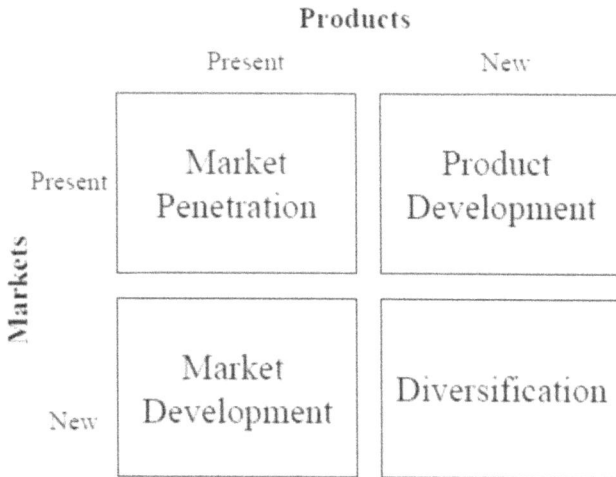

Integrative growth strategies

The two illustrations given earlier are classic examples of using integrative growth strategies. Most of the Indian companies which have been operating over last 40-50 years have used one of theses strategies some time or the other. There are four options which are available under this heading.

a. Backward integration: When a company decides to set up or acquire supply lines, it takes the form of backward integration. An organization decides to take this route for several reasons. They include assuring quality supplies, captive consumption, creating new SBU's and many others. Typical examples are given below:

• An engineering company acquires a foundry to manufacture castings

• A TV company sets up a manufacturing unit for TV-tubes

• A matchbox company sets up plantation which can

give them the type of wood needed for manufacturing match boxes

- A pharma company acquires a packaging unit needed for their medicines

It has been seen that several large organizations have set up their own businesses in areas like management consultancy, advertising agency, shipping, transportation and even starting their own financial companies. All these will fall under backward integration.

b. Forward integration: When a company decides to set up or acquire distribution lines, it takes the form of forward integration. An organization decides to take this route to ensure that their goods are reaching all the corners of the markets, prompt after sales service is available wherever required and so on. Typical examples are given below:

- A film producer takes over the distribution of his films so as to capture the market opportunities.

- A book publisher sets up a distribution organization so that the books reach all over the markets.

c. Horizontal integration: When a company decides to set up or acquire product lines which are in the same need satisfying markets, horizontal integration takes place. Typical examples are given below:

- A two wheeler company earlier manufacturing scooters, takes up the manufacture of motor cycles and mopeds. All products are thus in the business of meeting the 'transportation needs' of the markets

- A company manufacturing agriculture pumps, starts manufacturing industrial pumps for variety of applications. If they are manufacturing earlier centrifugal pumps and now they acquire a company manufacturing positive displacement pumps. With this, they can claim to offer the entire range of equipments in fluid handling.

- A company in print media only decides to enter the audio as well as audio-visual media. While they are still a media business, they have entered new media and that is why it will be horizontal integration.

d. Vertical integration: When a company manufacturing components and intermediates, decides to set up facilities to manufacture Original Equipments (OE) and/or finished goods. Typical examples are given below:

- A company manufacturing diesel engines takes up the manufacture of tractors.

- A company manufacturing bulk drugs takes up the manufacture of formulations.

- A printing press decides to enter in the business of publications of books

It must be noted that the integrative growth strategies will necessarily require capital investments. They will require new technologies, new products and also new markets. At the same time, it must be remembered that these strategies are integrated with the core business of the organization. These strategies will result in increase business opportunities and also, protection of the core business.

Diversification growth strategies

The organizations look for diversification on account of following factors:

- When they find that the present line of activity is declining for one reason or another. That would include changing tastes of customers, technological obsolescence and others.

- When they identify sunrise industries holding good potential for the future.

- The desire to become big with a wide portfolio of industries and thereby hold power and wealth

Undoubtedly, diversification strategies would require new investments in technology, new products and market mixes. The organizational will also have to develop the expertise to take on the new business. Theoretically, there are three options which are available under diversification strategies. They are,

a. Horizontal diversification: The organization comes out with new technologies. However, they may remain under a broad heading of same industry. For example, a company manufacturing electrical motors, starts manufacturing transformers. While they still remain under the heading of 'Electrical Equipments', the transformer manufacturing will require new facilities and different market segments.

b. Vertical diversification: Continuing with the same example of electrical motors, a company from small horse power motors takes up the manufacture of electrical motors up to 2000 horse power. It will require new capital investment, technology and will cater to a different market segment.

c. Lateral diversification: This is when an organization decides to enter in a line which is totally unrelated to its existing business. When India Tobacco Company (ITC) finds that the market for cigarettes is likely to decline, they enter in businesses ranging from hospitality (hotels), life styles (readymade garments) and many others. Reliance Industries starting with manufacture of polyester yarn enter in businesses like petrochemicals, petroleum, retailing, setting of Special Economic Zones (SEZ's) and oil exploration.

Every organization is interested in survival first and growth later. It cannot be left to chance. It will have to be properly planned. Using Ansoff's model, a more systematic approach can be undertaken. This will be the responsibility of the Strategic Management group of the organization. For small and medium enterprises, this will be the responsibility of the entrepreneur/promoter. The above write-up could be of use in identifying the alternatives.

OOO

6 | Breakeven Analysis

Many projects fail because of the poor planning, monitoring and control. This puts the precious resources under strain. We are giving three illustrations from the near past which we observed as management consultants.

Illustration 1: An express highway was planned between Pune and Mumbai some 15 years back. The earlier Mumbai- Bangalore highway called as NH4 was getting crowded, creating almost regular problems of traffic jam to the inconvenience of all. There was a 'Ghat Section' (Steep hill portion) which was the major bottle neck. Feasibility studies were conducted and it was decided that a 90 kms of express highway of world standard will be built. The earlier estimates suggested that it will cost close to Rs.1200 crores and will be completed in 3 years. Well known civil engineering companies were roped in. The calculations showed that a toll of Rs.52/- will be charged to passenger cars and higher toll charges to buses, trucks and other vehicles which will use the expressway. The project got delayed by more than 2 years; the cost got escalated to Rs.1800 crores. This resulted in the toll charges for a passenger car going to

Rs.80/ per vehicle. After 10 years of its operation, the expressway is yet to make profit and recently increased to toll charges to Rs.140/, much to the dislike of the users of the expressway. What went wrong with costing, execution of the project and monitoring?

Illustration 2: India is a big producer of Onions. They come in 2 varieties, the red and the white ones. The latter is priced higher. Nasik district in Maharashtra, and a place called Lasalgaon, can be considered as the 'Onion Capital' of India. Indian Onions have a good export potential. Saudi Arabia is a major importer of Indian Onions with a myth that it increases their libido! Onion has approximately 8 parts of water and 1 part of Onion. Hence, when we export onions, we are practically paying the freight to transport water. A technology was developed by Central Food & Technological Research Institute (CFTRI) using spray drying technology to convert the Onions in powder and flake forms. A manufacturing unit was set up at Nasik to manufacture Onion Powder with a capacity of 2 tonnes of finished goods per day. The production mostly was meant for export markets and a FOB price close to Rs.25/ per Kg was being realized. However, the company closed down soon. The post mortem analysis revealed that there were two reasons for failure. The first one was owing to the wide fluctuation of Onion prices. The project was envisaged when the raw material prices were less than Rs.2/ per Kg. The market showed the prices fluctuating widely between Rs.2/ to Rs.20/ per Kg. The second reason was more due to unethical reasons. The company in order to reduce the cost of raw materials started mixing white and red onions to make powder whose quality and color deteriorated and hence the export orders were rejected.

Illustration 3: The 'Open Sky Policy' of Government of India attracted large number of airlines to enter the market. The monopoly of Indian Airlines (Indian) ended when Jet air and Sahara entered the market. Then there was a spate of 'Low Cost Carriers (LCC)'. Before them, there were many like Modi Luft, East West Airlines, NEPC, Damania Airways and many others who had dared to enter this field and burnt their fingers. Why did they close down? And now there are LCC's like Air Deccan, Spice jet, Indigo and many others. A majority of them are faring poorly. Some like Sahara got acquired by Jet Air and, Air Deccan by Kingfisher Airlines. This trend is likely to continue. One should not be surprised if few more close down or get acquired/merged with bigger airlines. Why does this happen?

Do you see any pattern in these illustrations? They all have failed because they did not do proper Break Even Analysis (BEA). This is the management innovation which can be used by almost any and every organization. More so by the 'start ups' where BEA will guide them to chalk out their marketing strategies and efforts. This would be applicable to all types of organizations irrespective of their size, sector and nature of business.

Break Even Analysis

When asked to define what BEA is, most everybody incorrectly comes out with an answer that it is 'No profit, No losses. This does not exactly explain the principle and its application.

Definition: BEA is an exercise to find out the capacity utilization, occupancy and/or level of production, depending on the nature of business, at which income will equal total cost.

This can be expressed both in Algebraic as well as in Geometric form as shown elsewhere.

Algebraic expression

$$Y = m X + c$$

Where Y is income = Price x Volume. Y is a dependent variable.

Where m is a constant, expressed as variable cost per unit

Where X is a dependent variable, here expressing Volume

Where c is also a constant, expressing fixed cost

For BEA, Income = Total Cost

This is the level when 'there will be no profit and no loss'.

Price x Volume = Variable cost per unit x Volume + Fixed cost

Break Even Volume = (Fixed cost) / (Price – Variable cost per unit) = Fixed cost / Contribution

This is the most commonly used equation to calculate the break even volume. In order to do the calculations for BEA, we will have to understand the meanings of each terminology.

Price: It could be the price paid by the consumer (MRP), retail or wholesale price and for agricultural produce, it could be the farm price. In the illustrations given earlier, the price to use expressway will be the Toll, for agriculture produce, prices will vary at farm level, wholesale and retail level, as well a for institutional buyers. It will also vary with respect to seasonality. For airlines business, the price will be the fare paid by the passenger. (See the box to see different definitions of price)

BREAK EVEN ANALYSIS

Revenue

PROF IT

Total Cost

Variable Cost

LO SS

Fixed Cost

Break Even Point

NO. OF UNITS

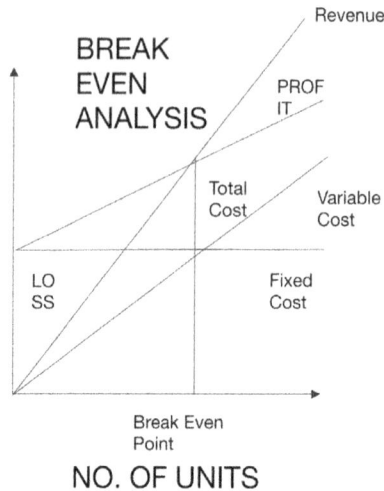

Price goes by many names

- Rent for an apartment, Tuition for education
- Fare for a train, Interest for a loan
- Tariff for electricity, Fee for a lawyer
- Toll on highway, Wage for a worker
- Premium for insurance, Commission to a salesperson
- Retainer by a consultant, Dues of alumni association
- Bribe by a government official, Salary for the executive
- Honorarium for faculty, Income tax for making money
- Dowry for the marriage, Khandani for extortion
- Match fixing by a bookie, Donation to a politician

Electing scoundrels is the price,

We pay for democracy.

Without it, life would have been so nice.

Fixed costs: These are the costs which do not vary in relation to either production or sales within a given range of plant capacity. They are incurred irrespective of volume of production. It must also be understood that investments in land, building, plant & machinery, technical know-how and other sundry assets are not the fixed costs. They are fixed assets. The costs incurred on maintaining them could be the fixed costs. Typically, from the Profit & Loss account of a Balance Sheet, we can find out which are the fixed costs. They would include:

- Monthly salaries paid to permanent employees
- Electricity & water charges paid for the administrative office
- Interest payable on term loans for creating fixed assets
- Insurance charges
- Maintenance charges on annual contract basis
- Administrative charges
- Overhead costs
- Depreciation

Variable costs: As the name suggests, these are the costs which are directly proportionate to the volume of production and sales. Given below is the list of variable costs which are incurred by businesses,

- Raw materials and other consumables
- Wages paid to workers related to volume of production
- Utilities (Electricity, water, steam, compressed air)
- Interest payable on working capital
- Maintenance costs on ad –hoc basis
- Marketing costs
- Sundry costs

Variable costs are also called Marginal costs. After the break even limit is reached, to produce one more unit, you will require only the variable costs. This concept is very effectively used in defining the capacities which can result in Economies of Scale, there by giving a competitive advantage. In Export Pricing, Marginal costing is invariable used by the organizations.

The sale at which the Income equals total cost is called Break even sales.

There are two more concepts which need to be known in relation to Break Even analysis. They are:

a) Margin of safety: It is the excess of present sales value over the break even sales value. Margin of safety is an indicator of the strength of the company. The greater the margin of safety, the stronger the company is.

b) Profit/Volume Ratio: The profit means Contribution and Volume means the sales value. It is generally expressed as a percentage. The higher the P/V ratio, the better is the performance. Profit links up both these concepts.

Profit= P/V ratio x Margin of Safety

Sensitivity analysis

As we have seen above, in order to calculate the break even volume, there are three variables at our disposal. They are the price, the fixed cost and the variable cost. Which of these three is the most sensitive affecting the break even volume? Going back to the illustrations given earlier, we will notice that,

Illustration 1: It was the fixed cost which was the most sensitive. Lack of control on the same, resulted in pushing the toll charges upwards and break even volume.

Illustration 2: It was the variable cost comprising of the raw materials and its fluctuations which resulted in the break even volume going up.

Illustration 3: The price was the most sensitive factor affecting the break even volume.

The following table presents these changes in a summarized manner:

Variables of BEV	Change	Effect	P/V ratio	Margin of safety
a. Price	a. Increase	Increases	Increases	Down
	b. Decrease	Decreases	Decreases	Up
b. Variable costs	a. Increase	Decreases	Decreases	Up
	b. Decrease	Increases	Increases	Down
c. Fixed costs	a. Increase	No change	Decreases	Up
	b. Decrease	No change	Increases	Down

From the above table, it can be seen that to improve P/V ratio, either selling price should be increased or variable cost per unit should be decreased. If price realization is higher, it will reduce the break even volume. If the fixed cost goes up, break even volume also goes up. If the variable costs go up, the break even volume goes up.

We are taking one example of a consultancy assignment which we recently undertook where the concept of BEA was the guiding factor to take decisions. Please refer to the box.

A Pune based company is in manufacturing variety of lamps which are used in different industrial applications. The company is highly innovative winning several awards from government and other bodies.

They identified a certain specialty lamp, namely 'Xenon lamp for medical endoscopy'. They got market survey done and found that presently the se lamps are imported at a price of Rs.150, 000/ and more. At this price, it is affordable only to large hospitals. Individual's medical practitioners cannot afford the same. The company spent over 6 months and developed the lamp matching the specifications of any leading brand from the world. They found that they had incurred the cost of close to Rs.20 lakhs on R& D which was considered as the Fixed Cost. The various components in it were costing around Rs.25,000/ or so. Now the crucial question they had was to find out what should be the Break even price? What factors will be the most sensitive in working out the break even analysis? The consultants gave the following advice.

a. Break Even Pricing: The market survey revealed that in Pune city alone, if the prices of the Xenon lamp is kept as shown, in order to achieve the break even, volume to be sold will be as shown. The all India demand was estimated at 1000 numbers per annum based on imports and consumption.

Assumed Price (Rs.)	B.E. Volume
• 75,000	40
• 50,000	80

- 40,000   133

It was decided that the price of this lamp in the Indian market will be kept at a base price of Rs.45, 000 /.

b. Sensitivity analysis: It was decided that a sensitivity analysis will be done under following assumptions,

i.   If the fixed costs rise by 10%

ii. If the variable costs rise by 10%

iii. If the price realization goes down by 10%.

The break even volumes were calculated again as given below:

Break even Volume (Nos.)

i.   With increased fixed cost   110

ii. With increased variable cost   114

iii. With reduced price realization   129

Thus, it was observed that the price will be the most sensitive factor which will have a bigger impact on the break even volume.

Practical utility of BEA

The concept of BEA has several practical applications, whether it is for a 'start-up' or for a 'running company'. They are given below:

- It helps in identifying the volume of production which must be sold to achieve the no profit, no loss stage. In other words, this helps in setting Goals and Targets which will first take care of all costs and later will result in profit.

- It helps in identifying areas where cost control can be effected to achieve the break even. For example, the organization can take such crucial strategic decisions as 'make or buy', commonly known as 'outsourcing'. They can look for alternative sources of supplies where the raw material costs will be lower, plan to reduce the costs like, electricity, marketing and others.

- BEA is invariably used for Forecasting.

- It helps in performance evaluation. When there are different divisions in the organization (SBU's), a comparison can be made.

- The BEA concept is so simple to understand that those executives who have no training in Finance can also put it to use.

- It helps the management in making decisions in many key areas such as the following:

- To study the feasibility of a project

- In pricing strategies for profit planning

- Allocation of orders between different factories

- Selection of economic manufacturing equipments

- Utilization of surplus capacity

- Method of manufacturing where there are two or more alternative processes available

- To run the plant or to shut it down

Thus, it can be seen that this management innovation is of immense use for any business. For a star hotel, airlines, restaurant, cinema theatre, it can guide at what level of occupancy, it can reach break even. For a manufacturing unit, it will tell at what level of capacity utilization, the break even volumes will be achieved. The organization then can make efforts to surpass this level and start making profit. It will then have to be ensured that the market has the capacity to absorb this volume at the price envisaged. Also, the organization must have adequate marketing efforts to achieve this volume of sales.

OOO

7 | Financial Analysis

A large majority of people shy away from the subject of Finance. Barring those who have studied the subject in college, the others feel that it is a tough nut to crack. Is it really so? Can we do without understanding the basics of Finance? The answer is certainly a 'No'.

The Finance Function

To put it very simply, Finance does mainly four functions. They are,

a. Money management: Everyone has to know that for their day to day operations, where does the money come from and where does it go? Whether it is for individuals/ families or businesses, irrespective of their size, sector or nature of business, this the commonest question which needs the answer. We will only consider it for a business organization. Whether it is a startup or a running business, the promoters/managers have to first look for Resource Mobilization. Money as one of the resources required for a business comes from two routes. They are Equity and Debt respectively. The funds raised by the promoters or obtained from the public through an Initial Public Offer (IPO) are called Equity. The funds which are raised from borrowings of any form from a term lending institution are called Debts. These funds which are collected for business purpose have to be utilized properly. This is called Resource Mobilization. These funds are used for creating Fixed Assets like purchase of land, building, technical know-how, plant & machinery and other sundry assets. For day to day operations, they are used for current assets, many time called as Working Capital.

b. Accounting: There are three branches of accounting. They are:

• Financial accounting: Daily accounting of all incomes and expenses have to be kept. This gives rise to preparation of Profit & Loss statement for a certain period as well as Balance Sheet on a certain day.

• Cost accounting: There are different cost centers which emerge while running a business. They may be for raw materials & other consumables, wages & salaries, utilities, administrative costs, maintenance, overhead, interest, depreciation and others. Proper accounting of these costs is necessary as it will help in deciding the price, allocation of budgets and deciding strategies on cost reduction.

• Management accounting: The first two types of accounting only takes care of maintaining the records for different account heads. The managerial accounting is assistance to decision making on such issues like make or buy decisions, deciding the alternative of raising finance which will be cheaper and so on.

c. Financial control: There are three areas which come under this heading. They are:

- Budgetary control: All well managed companies prepare their annual budget under different headings of income and expenditure. They then set up a proper monitoring and control system. This results in cost control, divisional control and other aspects.

- Capital expenditure control: Successful companies are always in an expansion mode. They undertake acquisition of fixed assets like land, building and other areas. The projects may get spread beyond a financial year. This exercise comes under this heading.

- Audits: In order to maintain transparency and legality, Audit is an integral part of every business. This is done internally through an Audit Department and through external independent auditors to ensure that proper accounting of all incomes & expenditures has been done.

d. Financial policies: Every organization has to take decisions in different areas of Finance. This could be regarding the capital structure, policies on depreciation, declaration of dividends, tax planning and many others. On some occasions, it becomes imperative to decide the policies to prevent sickness.

We hope that the readers will see that understanding Finance is not such a difficult thing. However, we must make it clear that this article is not on the subject of Finance. It is on Management Innovation and we are going to discuss one such tool under this heading which is of immense importance. It is Financial Ratio Analysis.

Financial Health of a Company

Like human beings, organizations too can become sick.

How to find out whether an organization is financially healthy or not? For that purpose, first we will have to define the parameters under which we will study the health of an organization. There are five important areas which need to be studied. They are,

a. Stability: The various questions which need answers are:

•   How strong and stable is an organization?

•   To what extent can it withstand the shocks caused by business cycles, risks and uncertainties?

•   What is the relative stake of the shareholders compared to the borrowings?

b. Liquidity: The various questions which need answers are:

•   How much cash is available with the company at any moment?

•   Can the company meet its liabilities like payment of wages & salaries, duties & taxes, interest due and others?

Perhaps, the most important aspect of any business is having adequate liquidity at all times. However, many organizations overlook this fact and the money is mostly locked under the heading of 'Receivables'. See box.

Late Ghanashyam Das (G.D) Birla was the founder of Birla Empire. Almost 60 years back, he explained the critical aspects of running a business. He used to say that in Birla Industries, the most important thing is 'Rokada (Cash). Then he made such a beautiful statement that 'If you have Rokada in your pocket, you are handsome, intelligent and can sing well too!'

Even today, most of the Birla Companies follow a system

which is called 'Padta'. This is based on the principle of Cash flow. This Principle ensures that every business transaction should result in a surplus cash flow to the company.

c. Management efficiency: We seldom observe that different organizations in the same business give different performances of excellence versus poor. Why does this happen? This is on account of the efficiency of their management of the businesses. The various questions which need answers are,

- How efficiently is the company managing its stock turnover, debtor's turnover as well as creditor's turnover?

- Is there any threat to the stability or liquidity of the company on account of such inefficient management?

d. Profitability: The prime objective of any business is to make profit. No one should have any objection to it. While profiteering is condemnable, profit is essential for the survival and growth of any business. The various questions which need answers are,

- How profitable are the company's operations?

- How much operating, gross and net profit the company has made during a certain period?

- What is the return on total capital employed as well as return on equity?

It was Pandit Jawaharlal Nehru who in the year 1952 had said that 'Profit in my dictionary is a dirty word' with reference to setting of Public Sector Undertakings (PSU). No wonder that most of the PSU's were making losses for a long time since their inception. However, the philosophy has undergone a change. Now, no body will deny the right of an organization to make a profit, including the PSU's.

e. Coverage: The funds for a business are raised through Equity and Debt respectively. Both need to be serviced. The questions which need to be answered then are,

*   Whether the business will be able to do debt servicing, first in terms of paying of interest and later by repaying the principle loan?

*   How the equity will be serviced through disbursement of dividends and then through the issuance of rights and bonus shares to create wealth for the shareholders'?

Use of Financial ratios- the innovative tools

We have no knowledge who developed these tools which offer immense practical utility as will be seen in the following paragraphs. We will be explaining different financial ratios which will be used to study the financial health of any organization and much more.

a. Financial stability: There will be two financial ratios which will be used to study the stability of an organization. They are,

*   Fixed Assets to Net worth:

    = (Fixed Assets at cost less depreciation)/ (Equity

    shares + Preference shares +Reserves & surplus)

This ratio gives the ownership of the organizational assets, how much of them have been funded by promoters' funds (Equity) and how much of them have been raised through borrowings (Debt). Lower the ratio, it shows higher ownership of the promoters. See box.

A general debate takes place as to which is the better route to raise funds for the project. Is it the equity or debt route? There are people who will have reasons to defend each alternative? If you raise funds through the Debt route, as soon as the funds are disbursed, the Interest starts. Many times the businesses are not in a position to take the interest burden. They fall sick. As against this, if the funds are raised through the equity, there is no compulsion to serve the equity which is done through declaration of dividend. Particularly, the start-ups may find it a better option as interest becomes liability. There is no compulsion as to when and how much dividend should be declared. Thus, the net profits can be ploughed back in the business. This is equally applicable to Foreign Direct Investments (FDI). We would like to take a different stand. We would recommend that a Debt is a better option than Equity. With proper financial discipline, after the loans are repaid, all the assets belong to the promoters. No wonder we hear of so many hostile takeover in the corporate world. You will see more and more companies buying back their own shares from the open market to consolidate their positions to thwart any such hostile takeover.

- Debt to Equity Ratio:

  = (Short term + long term liabilities including

    debentures)/ (Equity shares + preference shares +

    Reserves & surplus)

This ratio establishes the relationship between the borrowed funds and the shareholders' funds. A general belief is that no sane business man will start a business with his own funds. The risk is very high. On the contrary, if he borrows funds from a financial institution, his risk is reduced and he gets tax advantage on the payment of interest. As a thumb rule, we recommend a Debt to Equity ratio of 2:1 when the project commences. With proper debt servicing, this ratio should reduce over the years and may be in the fifth year, it should come down to 0.5 or so. This tells us that 'Lower the ratio, better is the financial health of the company.

b.   Liquidity: There are two ratios which are used under this heading. They are,

•   Current ratio= (Current assets)/ (Current liabilities)

By simple logic, we can see that this ratio should be more than 1. That means, the current assets are higher and can take care of all current liabilities. This means, higher is this ratio, more liquid the organization is. A desirable ratio is 2:1.

•   Quick ratio (Acid test ratio)

= (Current assets –Inventory)/ (Current liabilities)

It was noticed by the financial institutions that many organizations were showing a large inventory of raw materials as well as finished goods and also the receivables. They were borrowing against these current assets. This inflated the current assets but not necessarily their liquidity. Hence, as per Reserve Bank of India, stringent working capital norms were developed. A desirable ratio is 1: 1 but organizations are managing successfully with a ratio of 0.5 also.

c.   Management Efficiency: In order to have a healthy financial performance, management efficiency plays a crucial role. It is demonstrated by using three ratios as given below,

•   Stock turnover ratio

= (Cost of sales)/ (Average stock)

This ratio shows the efficiency of Inventory Management.

A low ratio may reflect a dull business. Average stock is obtained by divide the total of opening stock and closing stock by 2. A higher ratio shows better management. In our consultancy experience, we have observed stock turnover ratio of 250 (for bakery, 12 (for a 2wheeler manufacturer) and 5 (for Coal India Ltd.)

- Debtors' Turnover ratio

  = (Sundry debtors x 365)/ (Annual credit sales)

This ratio is expressed in number of days. It measures the efficiency in collection of debts. Every business man would like to keep this at zero. However, in a competitive world, this may not be possible and credit has to be given to customers. This further gives rise to the concept of 'Ageing of debtors' whereby we try to find out the outstanding and their duration. This way the impact of interest and erosion of profit can be calculated.

- Creditors Turnover ratio:

  = (Creditors x 365)/ (Annual credit purchases)

It indicates the extent to which the credit facilities are being enjoyed by the organization from its suppliers. It is also expressed in terms of number of days. A comparison between debtors' turnover ratio and creditors' turnover ratio indicates how efficiently credit is being managed on the whole, whether more credit is expended than received?

d. Profitability: All businesses are concerned about their bottom lines. There are two main ratios which can be used

- Gross profit ratio:

  = (Gross profit x 100)/ Sales Income

It indicates the gross margin obtained on all good sold. It demonstrates the efficiency in realizing a higher income and control over the costs. A higher ratio is always preferred.

- Net profit ratio

  = (net profit x 100)/ Sales income

It indicates the overall profitability after taking into account all expenses and incomes. This belongs to the shareholders' from which a part is distributed in the form of dividends and the surplus is transferred to Reserves & surplus account.

- Return on Total capital employed

  = (Net profit)/ (Total Capital employed)

It indicates the overall performance of the organization from the point of view of profitability. A higher ratio will be preferred.

f. Debt Service Coverage: The new philosophy is that 'taking a loan is not a sin but not servicing the debt is a sin'. This is measured by the following ratio,

- Interest Cover = (Profit before interest & tax)/Interest paid

A higher ratio is preferred which shows a good debt servicing.

Practical Utility

The data for using financial ratio analysis comes from two statements which appear in the annual report of a company. They are,

a. Balance sheet

b. Profit & loss statement

Any management tool must have a practical utility. Its use must help the organization in improving its performance.

The financial ratio analysis helps in the following areas,

- Trend analysis: Over last five years or so, the various financial ratios will be able to tell about the financial health of the organization, whether it is improving or deteriorating.

- Budgeting: The various ratios can be used while preparing the budget for the next year. In relation to the objectives set up, projected ratios can be worked out.

- Comparison with major competitors: The performance is always relative. A TV advertisement message asks the question ' Bhala Uski Kamiz Mere Kamiz Se Jyada Safed Kyon?' (Why is it that my competitor's performance is better than mine?) We have used this concept in areas of Competitive Intelligence. Armed with only the Balance Sheets of major competitors, we could give strategic advice to our client. SEE box.

- Comparison with generic industries: The various financial ratios can be compared with other industry players to obtain some strategic direction.

Inter Firm Comparison

This is a case of three companies all in manufacturing of Agriculture and Industrial Pumps. We collected the Annual Reports of these three companies for the same year and calculated the different financial ratios. Refer below:

	Company A	Company B	Company C
1. Sales (Rs. Million)	750.93	460.28	300.16
2. Current ratio	1.19(1)	1.28 (2)	1.62(3)
3. Quick Ratio	0.49(1)	0.57(2)	0.93(3)
4. Inventory Turnover	1.00(1)	1.03(2)	1.60(3)

Ratio (%)			
5. Debtors Turnover Ratio (Days)	110 (2)	161 (3)	95 (3)
6. GP / Sales (%)	4 (1)	6 (2)	9(3)
7. NP / Sales (%)	2.5 (1)	4.3 (2)	5.4 (3)
8. Return on Total Capital Employed	5.86 (2)	3.5 (1)	9.5 (3)
9. Earnings per Share (Rs.)	7.11	- 0.73	4.88
Total	11	16	21

Give 3 points for the best ratio followed by 3, 2, 1 for others in that order as shown in brackets. Then make a total of all the points. As can be seen, company A is the market leader. However, the best run company is C followed by company B. However, it also identified the areas where the market leader is weak in comparison to their major competitors where they had to improve. These were as follows:

- They must improve their current assets in comparison to current liabilities.

- They are carrying a large inventory resulting in lower inventory turnover ratio.

- The receivables are more. That means they must set up a better system for recovery of dues. This also could be happening because of their market mix. We found out that 80% of their business was coming from government sector where there are always problems of recovery.

- Because of all these factors, their profitability and return on capital employed was also low.

It can thus be seen that how a simple exercise can tell you about your financial position. It also tells you about your competitive performance and where the improvements need to be made. While we have discussed only 11 major ratios, there are many more which the readers' can refer from any good book on finance. Calculating a ratio is very easy. What is important is its interpretation. That is why this tool is considered as a management innovation to improve the performance of any organization

OOO

8 | Behavioral Theories

The world is full of different types of people. A few we find are highly motivated and do wonders. A majority of others blame it on the external factors, notably, their destinies for their failures. The latter have forgotten the saying that, 'Luck is the residue of diligence. The harder you work, luckier you get'!

The behavior of people in different walks of life has always fascinated researchers. This has given rise to several studies and management innovations which are useful to any and every organization. In this article, we plan to explore some of these tools and their utility.

Mayo's Hawthorne Experiments

George Elton Mayo was in charge of certain experiments on human behavior carried out at the Hawthorne Works of the General Electric Company in Chicago between 1924 and 1927. His research findings have contributed to organizational development in terms of human relations and motivation theory. Flowing from the findings of these investigations, he came to certain conclusions as follows:

- Work is a group activity.

- The social world of the adult is primarily patterned about work activity.

- The need for recognition, security and sense of belonging is more important in determining workers' morale and productivity than the physical conditions under which he works.

- A complaint is not necessarily an objective recital of facts; it is commonly a symptom manifesting disturbance of an individual's status position.

- The worker is a person whose attitudes and effectiveness are conditioned by social demands from both inside and outside the work

- Informal groups within the work plant exercise strong social controls over the work habits and attitudes of the individual worker.

- The change from an established society in the home to an adaptive society in the work plant resulting from the use of new techniques tends continually to disrupt the social organization of a work plant and industry generally.

- Group collaboration does not occur by accident; it must be planned and developed. If group collaboration is achieved, the human relations within a work plant may reach a cohesion which resists the disrupting effects of adaptive society.

The Hawthorne experiment was duplicated in one of the Tata factories on the insistence of another company manufacturing lighting fittings. See box.

The company manufacturing lighting fittings wanted to sell more of their products. They came up with a finding that productivity increases if the lighting in the factory is good.

They approached a Tata company with this proposal. The company requested scientific proof. It suggested that the experiment should be done in a separate shed where handpicked workers would be under observation. The project started with one tube light and the productivity at the end of the day was measured. Every day the lighting intensity was increased and the productivity was measured at the end of the day. On day 15, the lighting was at its peak. No wonder the productivity on day 15 was also highest. The company offering lighting fittings was happy that their hypothesis was proved right and hoped to get a large order. The management of Tata's wanted to continue the experiment further by going in reverse order. From day sixteenth, the lighting intensity was decreased, reaching zero on day thirtieth. The productivity was measured daily. What was the productivity on day thirtieth? To the surprise of all, it was higher than day fifteenth. This was a puzzle to all. How did this happen? The management interviewed workers one by one. The answers were amazing. Majority opined that they did not notice any change in the environment. As they were handpicked, they aimed at improving their productivity from the earlier day. That is why it was highest on day thirtieth than on day fifteenth! This experiment confirmed the findings of Hawthorne experiment: Self motivation is a bigger contribution to productivity than the external environment.

Abraham Maslow's Hierarchy of Needs

Abraham Maslow proposed in his 1943 paper, A Theory of Human Motivation his findings on his observations of humans' innate curiosity.

Maslow's hierarchy of needs, in its simplest form, is often depicted as a pyramid consisting of four levels as shown in the picture below. He said that a human being goes in to first satisfy his basic needs, called as Physiological needs. Once these are satisfied, he goes for the higher level defined as psychological needs. After these, come the Social needs and finally, the Self Actualization needs.

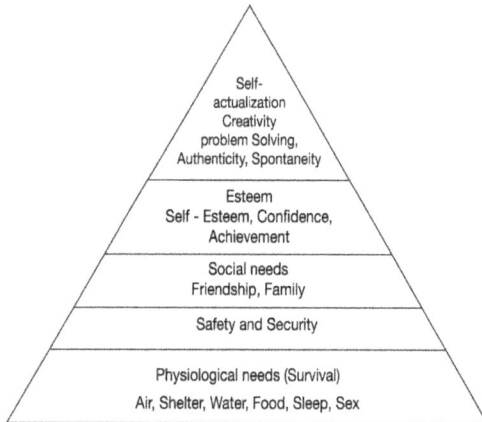

The physiological needs are defined in terms of hunger, clothing and shelter. The psychological needs will cover security, beliefs and anxieties. The social needs are of status, ego and other such aspects. The self-actualization needs talk about independence, self satisfaction and so on. This theory finds applications in almost every field besides in analysing the organizational behavior. One such example is given in the box.

Maslow's Hierarchy of Needs is used in marketing with an example of 'Chapati'. When a person is very hungry, he/she wants a Chapati and will care less about the type or condition of the chapati. However, once he is assured of Chapati, he may like to go for a particular Chapati like Alu Paratha, Rumali roti or Chapati made with Soyabin to reduce cholestrol. This is to fulfill his psychological needs.

When the same person goes to a five star hotel where the Chapati is priced say at Rs.25, it's not to satisfy one's hunger but to feed one's self esteem. Finally, if a person makes Chapati with his/her hands for a dear one, it is to fulfill the self actualization need. Marketers can use this concept in designing the messages for their products and services. It can also be used in deciding the product mix, price mix and distribution.

Herzberg's Motivational Theory

Fredrick Herzberg proposed the Motivation-Hygiene Theory, also known as the Two factor theory (1959) of job satisfaction. According to his theory, people are influenced by two factors:

Satisfaction, which is primarily the result of the motivator factors. These factors help increase satisfaction but have little effect on dissatisfaction.

Dissatisfaction is primarily the result of hygiene factors. These factors, if absent or inadequate, cause dissatisfaction, but their presence has little effect on long-term satisfaction

Motivator Factors
- Achievement
- Recognition
- Work Itself
- Responsibility
- Promotion Growth

Hygiene Factors
- Pay and benefits
- Company policy and administration

- Relationship with co-workers
- Physical environment
- Supervision
- Status
- Job security

Any management who is serious about investing in people and developing a great organization can use this innovation to gauge the satisfaction or otherwise in the organization. They can distinctly identify the Motivators as well as Demotivators. Corrective steps then can be taken accordingly.

McGregor's Theory X & Y

Douglas McGregor, an American social psychologist, proposed his famous X-Y theory in his 1960 book 'The Human Side of Enterprise'. Theory X and theory Y are referred to commonly in the field of management and motivation and still remain a valid basic principle from which to develop positive management style and techniques. McGregor's XY Theory remains central to organizational development, and to improving organizational culture.

McGregor's X-Y theory is a salutary and simple reminder of the natural rules for managing people, which under the pressure of day-to-day business are all too easily forgotten.

McGregor maintained that there are two fundamental approaches to managing people. Many managers tend towards Theory X, and generally get poor results. Enlightened managers use Theory Y, which produces better performance and results, and allows people to grow and develop. The theories are discussed in brief below:

Theory X ((Authoritarian management style)

- The average person dislikes work and will avoid it if he/she can.

- Therefore, most people must be forced with the threat of punishment to work towards organizational objectives.

- The average person prefers to be directed; to avoid responsibility; is relatively unambitious, and wants security above all else.

Unfortunately, we believe most Indian managers fall in this category.

Theory Y (Participative management style)

- Effort in work is as natural as work and play.

- People will apply self-control and self-direction in the pursuit of organizational objectives, without external control or the threat of punishment.

- Commitment to objectives is a function of rewards associated with their achievement.

- People usually accept and often seek responsibility.

- The capacity to use a high degree of imagination, ingenuity and creativity in solving organizational problems is widely, not narrowly, distributed in the population.

- In industry, the intellectual potential of the average person is only partly utilized.

In sum & substance, if adequate motivation is offered, even ordinary persons can deliver extra-ordinary performance. While money might be the best motivator for majority, after some time, it loses its charm. Then the challenges, passion and achievement motive drive people. It is then the responsibility of the superiors to give this motivation to their subordinates to obtain results. It is also the responsibility of the management to create the suitable environment.

Theory Z

Theory Z was not developed by McGregor, but by William Ouchi, in his book of 1981 'Theory Z: How American management can meet the Japanese Challenge'. William Ouchi is a professor of management at UCLA, Los Angeles, and a board member of several large US organizations.

Theory Z is often referred to as the 'Japanese' management style, which is essentially what it is. It's interesting that Ouchi chose to name his model 'Theory Z', which apart from anything else tends to give the impression that it's a McGregor idea. Theory Z essentially advocates a combination of all that's best about theory Y and modern Japanese management, which places a large amount of freedom and trusts with workers, and assumes that workers have a strong loyalty and interest in team-working and the organization.

Ironically, 'Japanese Management' and Theory Z itself were based on Dr. W. Edwards C. Deming's famous '14 points'. Deming, an American scholar whose management and motivational theories were rejected in the United States, went on to lay the foundation of Japanese organizational development during their expansion in the world economy in the 1980's. Deming was highly respected in Japan, which he rightly deserved. The award given by the Japanese government by the name Deming Award' is considered a prestigious one across the world.

The table below will show the difference which was recommended by Dr. Ouchi for American organizations.

Org Type A	Org Type J	Org Type Z
American	Japanese	Modified American
Short term employment	Lifetime employment	Long term employment
Individual decision making	Collective decision making	Collective decision making
Individual responsibility	Collective responsibility	Individual responsibility
Rapid evaluation & promotion	Slow evaluation & promotion	Slow evaluation & promotion
Explicit control mechanism	Implicit control mechanism	Informal control with explicit formalized measures
Specialized career paths	Non specialized career paths	Moderately specialized career paths
Segmented concern for employee	Holistic concern for employee	Holistic concern for employee including family

Intrapreneuring

Perhaps the pinnacle of motivational theories came when in 1985 Gifford Pinchot III came out with his book 'Intrapreneuring'.

An Intrapreneur is the person who focuses on innovation and creativity and who transforms a dream or an idea into a profitable venture, by operating within the organizational environment.

When a young person would like to select his/her career path, they have three choices viz:

- Managerial
- Entrepreneurial
- Intrapreneurial

Thus, Intrapreneurs are Inside entrepreneurs who follow the goal.

Each of the above have their advantages and disadvantages. A managerial career gives regular salary, growth prospects and less responsibility. At the same time, you always remain an employee following the dictats of superiors. Entrepreneurship gives freedom, an achievement motive, power and creation of wealth. At the same time, it requires your full attention, risk and chances of failure. Of the two, Intrapreneurship provides the best option. You can use the resources of an organization and help from other colleagues to come out with Innovation of any kind. However, this requires the efforts from both the sides. First, the employees will have to be self motivated and should be continuously thinking of innovation. Second, the organization must create the environment devoid of any red tape. It must encourage employees to form informal groups and come out with innovation. They are not punished even though, they may meet with failure. See box.

American company 3M is famous for creating Intrapreneurs. Some time back, they appointed a CEO from GE who was more keen on implementing Six Sigma in 3 M. Many scholars felt that 3M was moving away from their basic culture. When the said CEO shifted to Boeing, 3M was back to the culture of Intrapreneuring with telling effects. With this culture, every year they come out with close to 200 innovations. In Indian context, HCL and Thermax have vouched for the use of creating Intrapreneurs in their organizations.

We have studied these key developments in the area of Behavioral Sciences. These are management innovations which are relevant to every organization irrespective of their size, sector and nature of business. Further, they can also be used by individuals and families. Finally, it can be said that it is not the technology, product quality, price or the spend on advertising which brings results but the persons behind all this. Remember - 'A satisfied worker will always be more productive'.

OOO

9 | Theories in Economics

India and USA has something in common at the moment. Both are going through economic crisis. A severe recession is gripping both the nations. The causes of the same could be different for the two nations.

India is in serious economic trouble mainly due to following reasons:

- The inflation is raging and has touched the level of nearly 13 % in 2008 as per the figures released by the government.
- The world wide prices for a barrel of crude oil have touched USD 147 in 2013. In January 2015, they are around USD 50!
- The Government has liquidity crisis.
- Indian Rupee against USD is weak.

There are many other reasons for the downward trend of the economy. It is more than a month since the monsoon arrived. However, it has been found inadequate and the farming community is bearing the brunt of it. There is considerable power shortage across the country which is bound to hamper the industrial production. Some 5 month's back, Indian Rupee had strengthened against the USD and had reached a level of IR 39.13. This had affected the competitiveness of the IT industry. Now the USD has again appreciated and has touched close to IR 43.00. This has pleased the 'Exporter's Lobby'. But, what about the impact on over all economy?

The indicators are scary. Several industries like housing, automobiles, engineering, IT are showing signs of recession. The money position has become dearer and the rates of interest have gone up. The job market has also dried down. Many organizations are going for downsizing. The plight of the small scale sector, the ancillary industries is also bleak as their order positions have gone down. As compared to the average GDP growth of little over 8% last year, the agriculture sector is languishing at around 3% or so.

The budget 2008 had everything in it to boost the economy. The salient features included,

- Loan waiver of farmers to the extent of Rs.70, 000 crores or so.

- Raising the income tax limits for individual, women and senior citizen tax payers

- Budgetary allocation of several thousand crores each to various groups like BC/OBC, Minority and many others.

The treasury benches heralded it as a 'Dream Budget'. As expected, the opposition benches called it a 'Populist Budget' in view of the ensuing general elections. Now more than four months have passed and the Finance Minister (FM) and the Prime Minister (PM), who is an economist, are equally confused over how to steer the Indian economy. Most of the budgets in last several years have shied away from major issues. See box.

Most of the analysts criticize that no governments in last several years have touched on the following issues:

- The reduction in the government expenditure. Close to 70% of the nation's income is spent on the salaries of the staff. In spite of this, the productivity and the efficiency are always poor. Now the government is talking about implementation of the sixth pay commission. If that happens, the government expenditure will further increase.

- When Prof. Madhu Dandavate was the Finance Minister in the Janata Government from 1975-77, he did an exercise to estimate the black money in circulation in our economy. At that time, his estimate was close to Rs.500 crores. Now in 2008, it has exceeded Rs.500, 000 crores. This parallel economy is depriving the nation the use of this money. No government has come up with any serious measure to curb the black money.

- We want to have enhanced Foreign Direct Investment (FDI) in the country. However, the red tape, bureaucracy and corruption are the major impediments. While China has been getting FDI in excess of USD 50 billions year after year, India has to be contended with a little less than USD 4 billion annually. Why?

- The policies are seldom conducive to the industrial development. On one side, the customs duties are going down but the duties & taxes are not in the same proportion. This deprives the local industry any level playing field resulting in many of them closing down.

- It was in 1991 when Dr. Manmohan Singh was the Finance Minister; the government came with the plan of Privatization. Should it be the business of the government to be in business? There are bound to be differences of opinions. However, world over, the privatization has helped in improving the economies of the nation. Great Britain is one notable example. However, in India, bowing down to the political pressures, this exercise has been halted.

In this article, we have, therefore, decided to take up the Classical Economic Theories which evolved over the years. We will also make earnest efforts to see if they can provide us with some guidelines to improve the State of Indian Economy. We, however, would like to make it clear that we are not the students of Economics but of Management. Our approach may, therefore, sound simplistic.

Classical economics is widely regarded as the first modern school of economic thought. Its major developers include Adam Smith, David Ricardo, Thomas Malthus and John Stuart Mill. Sometimes the definition of classical economics is expanded to include William Petty, Johann Heinrich and Karl Marx.

Adam Smith's The Wealth of Nations in 1776 is usually considered to mark the beginning of classical economics. The school was active into the mid 19th century and was followed by neoclassical economics in Britain beginning around 1870.

Classical economists attempted and partially succeeded to explain economic growth and development. They produced their "magnificent dynamics" during a period in which capitalism was emerging from a past feudal society and in which the industrial revolution was leading to vast changes in society. These changes also raised the question of how a society could be organized around a system in which every individual sought his or her own (monetary) gain.

Classical economists reoriented economics away from an analysis of the ruler's personal interests to a class-based interest. Physiocrat Francois Quesnay and Adam Smith, for example, identified the wealth of a nation with the yearly national income, instead of the king's treasury. Smith saw this income as produced by labor applied to land and capital equipment. Once land and capital equipment are appropriated by individuals, the national income is divided up between laborers, landlords, and capitalists in the form of wages, rent, and interest.

Value Theory

Classical economists developed a theory of value, or price, to investigate economic dynamics. Petty introduced a fundamental distinction between market price and natural price to facilitate the portrayal of regularities in prices. Market prices are jostled by many transient influences that are difficult to theorize about at any abstract level. Natural prices, according to Petty, Smith, and Ricardo, for example, capture systematic and persistent forces operating at a point in time. Market prices always tend toward natural prices in a process that Smith described as somewhat similar to gravitational attraction.

The theory of what determined natural prices varied within the Classical school. Petty tried to develop a par between land and labor and had what might be called a land-and-labor theory of value. Smith confined the labor theory of value to a mythical pre-capitalist past. He stated that natural prices were the sum of natural rates of wages, profits (including interest on capital and wages of superintendence) and rent. Ricardo also had what might be described as a cost of production theory of value. He criticized Smith for describing rent as price-determining, instead of price-determined, and saw the labor theory of value as a good approximation.

Some historians of economic thought, in particular, Sraffian economists, see the classical theory of prices as determined from three givens:

- The level of outputs at the level of Smith's "effectual demand".
- Technology
- Wages

From these givens, one can rigorously derive a theory of value. But neither Ricardo nor Marx, the most rigorous investigators of the theory of value during the Classical period, developed this theory fully. Those who reconstruct the theory of value in this manner see the determinants of natural prices as being explained by the Classical economists from within the theory of economics, albeit at a lower level of abstraction. For example, the theory of wages was closely connected to the theory of population. The Classical economists took the theory of the determinants of the level and growth of population as part of Political Economy. Since then, the theory of population has been seen as part of some other discipline than economics.

Keynesianism and Keynesian Theory

It is an economic theory based on the ideas of twentieth-century British economist John Maynard Keynes. The state, according to Keynesian economics, can help maintain economic growth and stability in a mixed economy, in which both the public and private sectors play important roles. Keynesian economics seeks to provide solutions to what some consider failures of laissez-faire economic liberalism, which advocates that markets and the private sector operate best without state intervention. The theories forming the basis of Keynesian economics were first presented in The General Theory of Employment, Interest and Money, published in 1936.

In Keynes's theory, some micro-level actions of individuals and firms can lead to aggregate macroeconomic outcomes in which the economy operates below its potential output and growth. Many classical economists had believed in Say's Law, that supply creates its own demand, so that a "general glut" would therefore be impossible. Keynes contended that aggregate demand for goods might be insufficient during economic downturns, leading to unnecessarily high unemployment and losses of potential output. Keynes argued that government policies could be used to increase aggregate demand, thus increasing economic activity and reducing high unemployment and deflation. Keynes's macroeconomic theories were a response to mass unemployment in 1920s Britain and in 1930s America.

Keynes argued that the solution to depression was to stimulate the economy ("inducement to invest") through some combination of two approaches :

a. Reduction in interest rates.

b. Government investment in infrastructure - the injection of income results in more spending in the general economy, which in turn stimulates more production and investment involving still more income and spending and so forth. The initial stimulation starts a cascade of events, whose total increase in economic activity is a multiple of the original investment.

The New Classical Macroeconomics movement, which began in the late 1960s and early 1970s, criticized Keynesian theories, while "New Keynesian" economics have sought to base Keynes's idea on more rigorous theoretical foundations.

He also argued that to boost employment, real wages had to go down: nominal wages would have to fall more than prices. However, doing so would reduce consumer demand, so that the aggregate demand for goods would drop. This would in turn reduce business sales revenues and expected profits. Investment in new plants and equipment—perhaps already discouraged by previous excesses—would then become more risky, less likely. Instead of raising business expectations, wage cuts could make matters much worse.

Further, if wages and prices were falling, people would start to expect them to fall. This could make the economy spiral downward as those who had money would simply wait as falling prices made it more valuable—rather than spending. As Irving Fisher argued in 1933, in his Debt-Deflation Theory of Great Depressions, deflation (falling prices) can make a depression deeper as falling prices and wages made pre-existing nominal debts more valuable in real terms.

To Keynes, excessive saving, i.e. saving beyond planned investment, was a serious problem, encouraging recession or even depression. Excessive saving results if investment falls, perhaps due to falling consumer demand, over-investment in earlier years, or pessimistic business expectations, and if saving does not immediately fall in step.

Keynes findings are given below:

- Saving does not fall much as interest rates fall, since

the income and substitution effects of falling rates go in conflicting directions.

- Since planned fixed investment in plant and equipment is mostly based on long-term expectations of future profitability, that spending does not rise much as interest rates fall. Given the inelasticity of both demand and supply, a large interest-rate fall is needed to close the saving/investment gap.

- He argued that saving and investment are not the main determinants of interest rates, especially in the short run. Instead, the supply of and the demand for the stock of money determine interest rates in the short run.

- Because of fear of capital losses on assets besides money, Keynes suggested that there may be a "liquidity trap" setting a floor under which interest rates cannot fall.

- Saving involves not spending all of one's income. It thus means insufficient demand for business output, unless it is balanced by other sources of demand, such as fixed investment. Thus, excessive saving corresponds to an unwanted accumulation of inventories, or what classical economists called a general glut.

For Keynes, the fall in income did most of the job ending excessive saving and allowing the loan able funds market to attain equilibrium. Instead of interest-rate adjustment solving the problem, a recession

Criticism

The impact of Keynesianism can be seen by the wave of economists who have based their analysis on a criticism of Keynesianism.

One school began in the late 1940s with Milton Friedman. Instead of rejecting macro-measurements and macro-models of the economy, the monetarist school embraced the techniques of treating the entire economy as having a supply and demand equilibrium. However, they regarded inflation as solely being due to the variations in the money supply, rather than as being a consequence of aggregate demand. They argued that the "crowding out" effects discussed above would hobble or deprive fiscal policy of its positive effect. Instead, the focus should be on monetary policy, which was largely ignored by early Keynesians.

Monetarism had an ideological as well as a practical appeal: monetary policy does not, at least on the surface, imply as much government intervention in the economy as other measures. The monetarist critique pushed Keynesians toward a more balanced view of monetary policy, and inspired a wave of revisions to Keynesian theory.

Keynesian ideas were criticized by free market economist and philosopher Friedrich Hayek. Hayek's most famous work The Road to Serfdom, was written in 1944. Hayek taught at the London School of Economics from 1931 to 1950. Hayek criticized Keynesian economic policies for what he called their fundamentally collectivist approach, arguing that such theories, no matter their presumptively utilitarian intentions, require centralized planning, which Hayek argued leads to totalitarian abuses. Keynes seems to have noted this concern, since, in the foreword to the German version of the 'The General Theory of Employment Interest and Money', he declared that "the theory of aggregated production, which is the point of ['The General Theory of Employment Interest and Money'], nevertheless can be much easier adapted to the conditions of a totalitarian state [eines totalen Staates] than the theory of production and distribution of a given production put forth under conditions of free competition and a large degree of laissez-faire."

A study of these classical economic theories are relevant even today and can be applied by those who are at the helm of affairs to take the country out from the economic crisis in which we find ourselves.

Demand supply theory

Demand is the quantity of goods that buyers wish to purchase at a stated price. **Supply** is the quantity of goods that sellers wish to sell at a stated price. In general, the lower the price, higher will be the demand for goods and services. Given below is an illustration showing the demand and supply curves. The salient features of this model are given below:

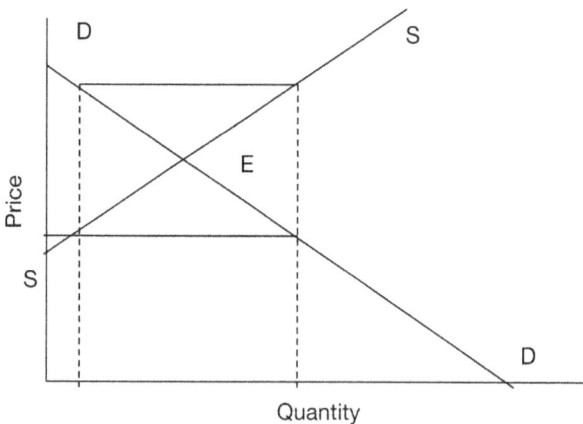

- The demand curve assumes that prices of other goods, incomes and tastes remain constant. The supply curve assumes that technology, price of inputs and degree of government regulation remain constant.

- At prices below equilibrium price E, there is excess demand which tends to raise price. At prices above equilibrium price, there is excess supply which tends to reduce price.

- An increase in the price of the substitute or a decrease in the price of a complementary product raises quantity demanded.

- An effective price ceiling may be set below the market equilibrium price to reduce quantity supplied and create excess demand until, or unless, the government contributes to supply.

This simple principle can very well be used to control the supply & demand of essential commodities. It helps in price setting, predicting responses to price changes, avoid surplus and deciding the optimum levels of supply. In 2008 the price of crude oil had reached a peak. See box.

How to overcome the fuel price rise?

- There are many ways by which we as the nation can combat the crisis of fuel hike. The question is, are we serious? Is the government serious? Given below are several alternatives to overcome this problem.

- A major expenditure is incurred on the government vehicles only. (Most of the time free of cost by the politicians and the bureaucrats. Watch the length of the caravan when any VIP visits the city!). If this can be curbed, it will result in major savings.

- The consumption of fuel goes up because majority of the vehicles are not properly tuned. The RTO/Police does not check the PUC certificates issued and we see many vehicles, mostly owned by the government,

---

throwing smoke on the streets.

- Encourage sharing of vehicles. In western countries, they are given preference on highways.

- In early 70s when a similar crisis had struck, European countries came out with a measure to ply even number vehicles on even days and odd number on odd days.

- Go for rationing of petrol/diesel thereby reducing the consumption. The petroleum companies will have to resort to 'De-marketing' instead of Marketing'.

- Develop hybrid vehicles and give them substantial subsidy so that more people will be interested in buying the same.

- Brazil has set the example where almost 50% blending of petrol/diesel is done with Ethanol. Unfortunately, in India, the petroleum companies are refusing to adopt the same. The sugar industry is asking for a rate of Rs.21/per litre which they are steadfastly refusing. If done, this will also improve the profitability of Sugar factories.

- Encourage oil exploration by giving incentives. We must reduce our dependence on imports and such wide fluctuations affecting our economy.

These are the alternatives to overcome the crisis. The question is whether we have the political will to do so?

Economies of scale

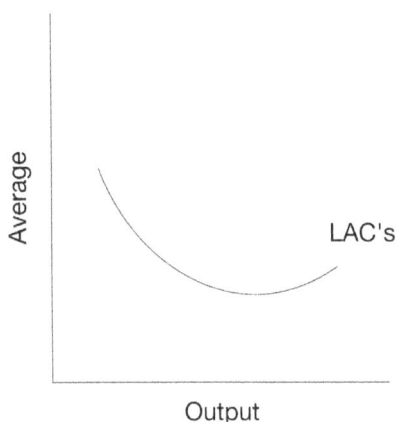

Economies of scale are increasing returns which are achieved when average costs (cost divided by output) decrease as output (the volume of production) rises. This principle needs to be applied to every sector including agriculture. The problem in India with agriculture is that the average land holding of the farmers' is hardly 2.1 acres. This does not give us the economies of scale and also deprives use of technology. This also does not give any competitive advantage to India. See box.

The price rise of essential commodities

The food grains, vegetables, fruits and all other essential commodities have reached the skies. Why has this happened? Is this shortage real or artificially created? It ahs been the experience in the past that whenever the elections are round the corner, this situation emerges. It leaves a reasonable doubt in the minds of the common man that this is owing to the nexus between the politicians and the trading community. It ha snow been proved that the government machinery is incompetent to manage the

---

system. The Public Distribution System (PDS) is good example which is full of corruption.

When the shortages occur, the imports become essential. On one side we talk about record production of food grains and on the other side we import sub-standard wheat, that too at a higher price! Who gets kickback is obvious but the guilty is never punished. The poor man suffers.

Elasticity of demand

Elasticity measures the sensitivity of demand or supply of goods to percent changes in the price of those goods or to changes in the income available to purchase those goods. Quantity of goods demanded and supplied varies with changes in prices of those goods, changes in prices of other related goods and changes in the available income. The rise in fuel prices will see a reduction in demand. This model also helps in price setting and predicting responses to price changes.

Economics has been described as the Mother Science of all the Sciences. At the same time, it leaves many unanswered questions. In a lighter vein, it is said that all economists agree to disagree. They come out with models and predictions. And then with explanations, why they have not come out true!

OOO

10 | Marketing Analysis

- Very few organizations look ahead in the future. In majority of the organizations, long term planning does not exist.

- Those organizations that plan for one or more years, very seldom they set up a system for monitoring their performance periodically.

- If it is a multi-product, multi-market company, product line contribution analysis is generally available. However, the same in terms of different product types, brands and packaging is seldom done.

- Few companies are aware about the contribution made from different geographical markets. This may be for domestic as well as for the overseas market, different zones, regions and states in the domestic markets.

- However, very few organizations do a thorough analysis with respect to end users, channel members and individual sales persons.

- Many organizations may know how much they are spending on Marketing. However, a majority do not know how much they have spent on marketing sub-functions like market research, advertising, sales promotion and field selling to name a few.

- Very few organizations carry out comparison with their major rivals with respect to incomes, expenses and others.

Modern marketing has been defined as a civilized form of warfare. This war will be intensified in the era of globalization. This will require regular analysis of performance, monitoring and control to achieve the organizational objectives.

Winning with Analytics

American management innovators are many times accused of putting Old wine in new bottle. One such new tool is now being talked about. In an increasingly competitive and rapidly changing business environment, the key to successful decision making lies in being better informed and being able to correctly interpret the abundant volume of trends, data and statistics floating around. This tool is being called 'Analytics'. American management Guru's come to India and conduct training programs charging fat fees. Is it really worth it? (India Today September 1, 2008).

There is another saying that 'it is easy to make simple things look difficult, but it is not so to make difficult things look simple'.

We are, therefore, discussing some simple analytical tools in this article. These can be used by any organization to analyze its own performance to decide the future course of action.

Sales Analysis

This is one of the simplest tools that can be put to use to evaluate the performance. This is more essential for a company which can be described as a Multi-product, Multi- market company. Without this, the company may not know from where the profit is coming and where are they losing. Sales analysis is an exercise in analyzing the sales with respect to different variables. The variables are as follows:

• Products: The product mix of a company comprises of different product lines, product types, brands and packaging. The periodic review can assist to define which are the company's star products, cash cows, question marks and dog products. The model BCG Product Portfolio Management discussed earlier can be put to use for strategy formulation.

• Territories: A company has to keep on expanding its market from local to regional, from regional to national and finally from national to international markets. However, what is the contribution from each market must be known so that what marketing efforts are needed can be decided? What is the contribution of domestic market versus exports; contribution from four zones, different states and even going down to the contribution from each district in India can be ascertained?

• End users: Particularly, in Industrial Marketing, the customers belong to different end user segments. What is the contribution of each end user is important to know to define Target Customers. At the same time, it must be understood that the target markets are also affected by environmental changes. Hence, the target market definition has to be redone and thus the need for proper analysis. In Consumer Marketing, the analysis will reveal the consumption data with respect to the demographics in terms of age, gender, income, education and profession.

- Channels: The goods & services can be delivered to the end users directly or by using different channels of distribution.

The information and analysis on how much business is generated by different channel members is essential. A company may have different zonal & regional offices and it becomes imperative to evaluate the contribution of each office to decide whether to continue with a particular office or opening of new offices.

The Information technology can assist in this analysis. There are readymade software's available for this purpose. Software named SMART (Sales & Marketing Analysis & Review Technique) can be put to use. See box.

We are taking an example of a pharmaceutical company, which makes close to 40 different types of medicines. They are available in four different packaging namely, Liquids, Tablets, Capsules and Injectibles. How will the use of SMART look?

Product line contribution analysis: The contribution of each product type and packaging over the years will give the trend. It will also tell which packaging form is more popular.

End user analysis: The company has major sales through channels and substantial sales directly to institutional buyers. It may happen that the latter may give volumes but at reduced profit margin.

Territory contribution analysis: It is essentially to know what is the contribution of domestic markets and shares of four zones, regions, states and districts. Similarly, what are the export sales, to which countries and the trends can be analyzed?

Sales person contribution analysis: An average size pharma company uses around 200 field sales representatives. It is very important to know what is the contribution of each to decide the rewards for the performers and to give a boot to non-performers.

Channel contribution: The pharma company uses close to 150 distributors, 500 stockiest and close to 100,000 retailers across the country. They would like to reward those who are doing a better job than others. This will be possible only through proper analysis.

Prescription audit: Worldwide, pharma companies use prescription marketing. In other words, the sales persons of the company visit the medical doctors and try to convince them to prescribe their products. Those doctors who are supportive, can be given incentives in different form.

It can thus be seen that how critical it is to have this kind of analysis. Another example can be given of leaders in Pump Manufacturing- Kirloskar Brothers who used to manufacture 20 types of pumps, in 30 different sizes, in 6 materials of construction, using 2 prime movers, namely, diesel engine and electric motor and catering to some 30 different market segments. With so many variables, a proper analysis becomes a 'must'.

Analysis

The above analysis can be put to use for following

Strategic Decisions:

- To find out whether the 80:20 (Pareto) concept will be applicable or not.

- To identify the major product lines, types, packaging and brands, which give the company its Bread & Butter.

- To decide discontinuance of product lines which are not contributing any more.

- To decide policy on production planning and inventory control.

- To decide how the sales force, distribution effectiveness can be increased further. The non-performers can be given warning to improve their performance or leave.

- To develop Relationship Marketing with key customers to ensure their retention.

- To decide the marketing efforts needed to achieve the objectives

- To carry out variance analysis with respect to Target and Achievements.

Profitability analysis

The above analysis can be further extended with respect to profitability in terms of products, territories, end customers and also in terms of order lot. This will be particularly useful in taking decisions on Exports. If the company has already achieved the Break Eeven in domestic market, then, they can decide the pricing strategies for the export markets. Principles of Marginal Costing & Pricing can then be considered in order to make a penetration in international markets.

Market share analysis

The performance is always relative. In a competing economy, it is also measured in terms of market share and its growth over the years.

The market shares are generally of two types viz,

Total market share: In a particular industry, we will consider the Brand Competition, which is offered by similar products. This could be for the entire geographical market, zones, regions and districts.

Served market share: A company may not be operating in a total market but only in a served market with respect to territory, end use segments or class of products. In that case, only the market share in that served market will be calculated. See box

---

Illustration: In the year ended March 31, 2014, some 24,50,000 passenger cars were manufactured in India. Mercedes Benz produced close to 7200 cars. This will give them a market share of hardly 0.3 %. This is their total market share. The car market is differentiated as small, mid size sedan, executive class and luxury cars. The latter can be considered in price range over Rs 20 lakhs per vehicle. There were close to 20,000 cars that were sold in the premium segment in India giving Mercedes Benz a market share of 34%.This is their served market share.

This way it is possible to calculate the market shares in a Niche Market where the company would like to operate. They can then decide their strategy of first retaining their existing market share and later planning strategies to expand the same.

Marketing Expense Analysis

No company can achieve any results unless and until they put in adequate marketing efforts. This marketing effort could be on product differentiation, marketing communication, field selling, setting channels of distribution, providing before & after sale services and any others. It is a simple economic phenomenon that the revenue increases with increasing marketing efforts. However, it must be realized that it cannot keep on growing forever. The Law of Diminishing Returns is then applicable. Every organization thus wants to know what marketing efforts they must put in to get the optimum results. This is not an easy task and requires continuous monitoring.

The analysis of marketing expenses for different types of companies presents an interesting picture. Typically, the Industrial marketing companies spend approximately 5% of their income on marketing. This is because they have few customers to cater; they do not require costly media advertising as the same is achieved through personal selling. In comparison, the Fast Moving Consumer Goods (FMCG) companies spend as much as 35% of their income on marketing. This is because of the huge costs which are involved on mass media, the commissions which are payable to the channel members, transportation, inventory control and many others.

The Services Sector companies spend approximately 10% of their income on marketing. All marketing efforts are eventually defined in terms of expenses expressed in terms of Rupees. This gives rise to an interesting tool called Marketing Ratio.

We are all familiar with different types of financial ratios like Debt to Equity ratio, Current ratio and others, which were covered in an earlier article by us. What is a Marketing Ratio?

Marketing Ratio: Any marketing expense expressed, as percentage to income is a marketing ratio.

Marketing ratio = (Marketing Expense / Sales Income) x 100

The marketing expenses are broadly classified under the following major sub-heads:

Market research expenses: The expenses incurred in collection of all types of market information will come under this heading. It could be for secondary sources like subscription to journals, databases and others as well as for primary research on travel costs, field costs, administrative & overhead costs and compensation to researchers.

Marketing communication expenses: A wide range of expenses is covered under this heading. It will include expenses on Advertising (Production & media costs. The latter will include print, audio, audio-visual, outdoor, post as well as Internet as media). Publicity which will include the cost of organizing a press conference, retaining a public relations agency for company's products, people and performance publicity and finally expenses incurred on Sales Promotion. The last one includes a variety in terms of organizing events, participation in trade fairs, organizing seminars, designing schemes for consumers as well as dealers, just to name a few.

Field selling expenses: This will include the cost incurred on the travel of sales force, their lodging & boarding, local conveyance, free samples to be given and any other out of pocket expenses.

Market logistics: In globalized and highly competitive environments, this has become one of the major expense head, which requires proper monitoring and control. This will include such costs like setting of warehouses, transportation, packing & forwarding, loading & unloading, insurance; inventory carrying costs and many others depending on the type of business. For perishables, this will also include the cost of damaged goods.

Service costs: With rising competition, all products are looking the same and the prices are almost on par, it is the Service Element in Marketing which has become most crucial. This also determines the competitive advantage a company can have over its rivals.

However, the Service comes with a cost. They can be classified as Before Sales Service and 'after sales' Service. The former may include communication, trial, guarantee, raising of fiancé, installation and other such costs. For the latter, they will include warrantees, supply of spares, returned goods and other costs.

There are as many as 45 Marketing Ratios, which we have identified. Now the question is how we make use of Marketing Ratio Analysis. An illustration will make it clear. See box.

In one of our consultancy assignments, we used this concept. There are two companies manufacturing Pumps. We compiled this data from their Annual report. Refer next page

		(In Lakh rupees)
	Company A	Company B
• Sales income	2000.00 (100)	8000.00 (100)
• Net profit	200.00 (10)	80.00 (1)

- Advertising   10.00 (0.5)   80.00 (1)
- Publicity   10.00 (0.5)   8.00 (0.1)
- Sales promotion   40.00 (2)   40.00 (0.5)
- Field selling   100.00 (5)   80.00 (1)
- Debtors'   45 days   120 days

Note: The figures in bracket give percentages to the income.

Inference:

1. Company B is the market leader and 4 times bigger in revenue generation. However, the company A makes more profit as a percentage compared to company B. This is on account of its well-defined marketing strategy and allocation of expenses.

2. Both are in Industrial Marketing. Company A is spending less on advertising but more on publicity, sales promotion and personal selling as compared to company B which is obviously paying them rich dividends.

3. Company A has managed its debtors at only 45 days while company B has debtors amounting to 120 days. This results in erosion of their profitability.

4. An inter-firm comparison of marketing expenses throws light on what policies need to be adopted to improve the performance.

Applications of Marketing Ratio

The use of Marketing Ratios serves the following purposes:

Attitudinal Tracking

The customer needs & wants over the years are changing. It is very important for every organization to do a regular check on these changing habits. Or else, a company may find itself out of business. Given below are few illustrations, which display attitudinal changes, affecting many industries:

- More persons now prefer to eat outside than cook food at home giving opportunities in fast food business.

- The readymade garments are more preferred over going to tailor to get clothes made.

- Home viewing of feature films is more common than visiting multiplexes and spending lot of money on tickets, parking and snacks.

- Motorcycles are now more popular than scooters and mopeds.

- Cellular phones are more in use than the landline phones.

These and many other changes will have to be noted and used for new products development and strategy formulation.

Marketing Audit (MA)

We have all heard of Financial Audit. But, what is a Marketing Audit? The financial audit is a statutory requirement for all registered organizations, whether they are partnership, private or public limited or co-operative organizations. It ensures proper accounting of income & expenditures. It does not go beyond it. Marketing Audit could work as an overall evaluation of the performance of an organization even though it is not so commonly used. It is because it is a very exhaustive and costly exercise. The expertise needed also is limited.

Definition: Marketing Audit has been defined by Philip Kotler (Marketing Management 11 th Edition) under three heads, namely,

a) It is a comprehensive, systematic, independents and periodic review of,

b) A company's marketing environment, planning, strategy, policies, organization and others.

c) To identify problem area and to come out with recommendations on improving the marketing performance of an organization.

Naylor & Wood in their book 'Practical Marketing Audits' go a step further. In addition to the above, they say that Marketing Audit helps in improving the profitability of the company. No other management tool talks about this objective.

Components of Marketing Audit

Following major components of Marketing Audit have been identified. They are,

a) Marketing environment audit: This will study the demography, economy, technology, polity and cultural changes under the heading of Macro environment. In addition, it will study the markets, customers, competitors, channels, suppliers, facilitators and publics under the Task environments.

b) Marketing strategy audit: It will review the company's vision & mission statements and the strategies sued to fulfill them.

c) Marketing organization audit: This will evaluate the organization structure, functional efficiency and interface efficiency in the organization.

d) Marketing systems audit: Under this, it will evaluate the marketing information system, marketing planning system, marketing control system and new product development system to name a few.

e) Marketing productivity audit: This will review the company's profitability analysis and cost effectiveness analysis.

f) Marketing functions audit: This will evaluate the effectiveness or otherwise of a company's products, pricing, distribution, advertising & sales promotion, positioning and sales force strategies.

A Marketing Audit requires obtaining frank feedback from all those who are operating in the marketing system of a company. This will include internal customers like employees at all levels and external customers, which will include consumers, customers, channel members, suppliers, facilitators, shareholders, financial institutions, government agencies and finally the general public's.

We have been steadfastly maintaining that all these management innovations contribute to the knowledge. And 'the essence of knowledge, is having it, is to apply it'.

OOO

11 | Competitive Intelligence

What is common between the following?

- Kargill
- 9/11
- Attack on Indian parliament on December 15

In last few months, there have been terrorist attacks in India at Jaipur, Varanasi, Bangalore, Ahmedabad and the latest at New Delhi. It has resulted in loss of property and lives. The culprits have not been caught, as yet. In all these mishaps, the common thing was 'Intelligence Failure'.

Kargill: The Pakistan soldiers infiltrated in Drass- Kargil sector in the J&K area and we had no knowledge about it. And if we had, we did not act on it. Thousands of our brave soldiers lost their lives. The government set up investigations for this debacle that came out with one single conclusion that it was intelligence failure!

9/11: The Islamic terrorists decided to strike at three of the most powerful centers in USA. First, it was the commercial power of the USA symbolized by the twin towers of World Trade Centre. Second it was Pentagon, the symbol of its military power. Finally, it was White House where President of USA resides. The terrorists succeeded in striking the first two targets but were overpowered in the third attempt. The US government also set up a committee to investigate which came out with a conclusion that it was nothing but intelligence failure. The entire world wondered that how could the only super power, the United States of America could have such an intelligence failure?

12/15: When the Indian parliament was in session, the terrorists dared to attack it. Several security personnel and also few terrorists were killed. Some were arrested. As usual, a committee was set up to investigate which came out with the conclusion that it was an intelligence failure. More than six years have passed and the terrorist captured is yet to be punished for his act of treason!

Unfortunately, the attacks have not ceased. On the contrary, their frequency has intensified. The police and all the agencies involved in curbing the terrorist activities are at a loss as to how to prevent them. The conclusion is simple. Our intelligence wing is not strong enough to prevent these dastardly acts.

What is intelligence?

The illustration given below shows the hierarchy of market intelligence. It begins with data collection. There is no market or product on which data is not available. However, all this data may not necessarily be of use to us. When we put this data in a structured format and usable, it becomes information.

The dictionary defines information as knowledge which is communicated by others or obtained through studies and investigations. We are in the information age but all the information may not be useful to us. The one which can be put to use is knowledge. Knowledge gives us insight about a particular industry, market or products. However, it must be noted that data, information, knowledge and insight is something which has already happened. If we use it, it will be called 'Post Mortem Analyses. What we require is information and knowledge on the future. How can we obtain it when it is yet to happen? This is where intelligence comes in play. And finally, with experience, the peak is achieved with wisdom.

HIERARCHY OF MARKET INTELLIGENCE

WISDOM

INTELLIGENCE

INSIGHT

KNOWLEDGE

INFORMATION

DATA

There is no business on earth, whether for profit or non profit, where there is no competition. We are exposed to competition right from our childhood days. We compete with our siblings to attract the attention of our parents.

When we join school, we have to compete with our classmates in studies and in sports. When we take up a job, we have to compete with our colleagues for promotion. In business, we have to compete with the other players in the market. The monopolies enjoyed by few businesses in India few years back have vanished. The modern marketing is defined as a civilized form of warfare. A survey done in India of some top 1300 CEO's revealed that the most critical factor in managing businesses in the years to come will be the Competition.

The million-rupee question then is how to outsmart, out surpass and out maneuver you competitor? A new corporate discipline called Competitive Intelligence is now available which you can easily use in your business, in any business.

The business scenario

Till 1980 in India, the competition was almost non-existent or was minimal. Most of the businesses enjoyed a near monopoly. After 1984, the situation started changing when government announced the policy of "Broad banding". 1991 was the landmark year when India liberalized. The imports were permitted, the customs duties were reduced, new players entered in the market, the existing players were allowed to expand capacities and launch new products. The customers became demanding and for the first time they started getting a choice. It became a free for all. For businesses, first, it was the survival and then you could think of growth.

We witnessed some competitive wars in the Indian markets in last few years.

a. Soap wars, Lux competing against Rexona

b. Two wheeler wars, Bajaj competing against Hero Honda

c. Cola wars, Cocoa cola competing against Pepsi cola

d. Mint wars, Polo brand versus other, the mint with a hole and the whole mint.

e. Political wars, BJP versus Congress.

f. Low cost air carriers competing against established airlines like Indian, Jet Air and now Kingfisher.

The list is not exhaustive. We have already started witnessing the competitive wars for many other products. This includes Banking, Insurance, Public Transport, Media. TV channels and many more.

The importance of Competitive Intelligence, CI for short, is being understood mainly for the following reasons:

a. There is no individual or business where there is no competition.

b. The competition comes in different shapes and sizes. It comes from similar and substitute products, it comes from domestic as well as foreign players, and it comes from organized as well as from the unorganized sector. For few products, even today, it comes from smuggled goods. How can a business fight so many different types of competitors?

c. The businesses are becoming complex. You have multi product and multi market companies. For each product and for each market, you could have a different competitor.

d. The information age is here and the technology has helped in managing intelligence.

Scope of CI

Most of the businesses think that they already know about their competitors. Why will they require CI? Is it really true? The answer is far from the truth. Let us see what intelligence they require:

-   Who are their major competitors?

-   What information do they have on their competitors?

-   What are their strengths & weaknesses?

- How did they collect the information?
- What is the response of the competitor when they make any changes?
- How will they use this information in formulating their business strategy?
- Are they using competitive intelligence as a tool to score over their competitors?

It is quite likely that everyone thinks about tackling the competition in their own way.

Myths on CI

We would like to blow some of the myths associated with the CI.

1. CI and market research are not the same: Market research is a systematic exercise in data collection, analysis of relevant data, drawing conclusions and offering recommendations on any marketing problem under consideration. However, the data collected has already happened. It does not tell us anything of the future. CI is futuristic.

2. CI is not spying: We do not deny that espionage does not take place in industry. But, it has been established that CI is perfectly legal and ethical.

3. Data, Information and intelligence are not the same: In the illustration shown earlier, we have already differentiated between theses terminologies. Intelligence does not mean reams of data. On the contrary intelligence could be very short to give us a warning.

4. Competitive and competitor intelligence is not the same: There is a Competitive environment which is changing rapidly. It can affect the Competitiveness of

any company. It may not have anything to do with Competitors. For example, some years back there was 'Bird Flu' in certain parts of India. It affected the poultry industry very badly. Lakhs of birds had to be killed, the consumption of poultry products went down substantially. This did not happen due to competition. As against that, the competitor intelligence will deal with competition from similar as well as substitute products. Scooters faced competition first from Mopeds and then from Motor Cycles.

5. There is no information available on small and private companies: This is not true. It is very much possible to obtain information on any and every organization.

6. Information is free: Every information has a price tag now. It has created a big market for information. At the same time, it is also not true that it is very costly.

7. CI is an IT product: Technology is also playing a major role. Many IT companies have launched CI products, as they claim. However, we believe that CI cannot be a product but a process.

8. You do not have all the information you wanted: We think that we have all the information which we wanted. This is not true. The quote by Alvin Toffler in his book 'The Third wave' will make it clear. He has said that' All managers have realized that the information which they have is not what they want, information which they want, is not what they need, and the information which they need is seldom available.

9. Not every decision requires CI: There is a general belief that CI is more needed by marketing people. This is not true. It will be required in every functional area of R &D, Manufacturing, finance, HR and others.

10. CI requires substantial investment: This is not true at

all. It does not require any investment in hardware as well as in software. All it requires is a change in the mind set of the people. All they have to do is to keep their eyes & ears open to gather any small piece of information which can be of use to them.

11. CI does not bring any tangible benefit: Some people may think that CI is a waste of time. It may not bring any tangible benefits. However, we cannot think of any other discipline which can be used in formulating the short term as well as the long term strategies for any organization.

We hope that the above eleven points will clarify what CI is not.

It is surprising that so many people are still not thinking about the competition they are facing presently and will be in the future. It is at all levels. India is competing as a nation with at least 40 other developed and developing countries of the world, the state of Maharashtra has to compete with other 6-7 states to attract the industrial investment, every district is competing with others for same purpose and certainly the businesses are having a fierce fight with one another. Do the Central, state and local governments in India use CI? We do not think so. Otherwise, Tata's would not have faced the problem which they did in selecting Singur in West Bengal to make Nano cars?. See box.

> Our research reveals that the government's in USA, Canada, UK, Australia and Japan are the leading nations which use CI to help their companies when they decide to go overseas. Enron is a classic case of the use of CI in 1991. India had liberalized its economy. Many projects were given priority. One such was in Power Generation.

Government set up fast track clearances in infrastructure development projects. At that time Enron was going great guns. They also had the support of US government. It is generally believed that Central Intelligence Agency (CIA) of the USA helped them in venturing in India. What did this include? Their first job was to find out the persons who would be the decision makers. This was not difficult. However, the second information was more critical in nature. This was to find out their weaknesses. What will be their response to the 3W's, that is, Wine, Wealth and Women?

Enron became a case study, first in B-Schools as a success story. When they declared bankruptcy and were known world over as a Rogue Company, it again became a case study in B-Schools under the heading of Business Ethics. The authors have written a case study on Enron which was used at a training program of senior IAS officers at the prestigious Tata Management Training Centre (TMTC) in Pune in July 1985.

Then what exactly is CI?

There will be no organization on earth which does not face the following situations:

- A new entrant from India or overseas comes in the market all of a sudden who has better resources than you?

- Your existing major competitor launches a new product or reduces their prices by 25 per cent?

- Two of your senior managers resign and join your competitor?

- Your dealers switch their loyalty and start trading with your rival's products?

- Your major competitor comes out with an advertising campaign in which they make fun of you?
- A small-scale manufacturer copies your product and starts selling at 50 per cent lower price?
- Government is planning to ban some of your products which have been found to be hazardous?

All businesses are facing these situations daily. What should they do? This is where CI can come to their help. Let us see what CI can do for them

a. Competitive research and reconnaissance: This aims at getting answers to the basic questions on who is my competitor, what are his strengths & weaknesses, what are his strategies, what is his reaction to your strategies and so on so forth. This information is not going to fall in your just like that. This will require setting up a system and procedure for periodic collection of data.

b. Analysis of the data: The analysis of data will help you in the following manner,

i) Early warning system: With CI, you will be able to tackle the situations which were described earlier. Or, otherwise it will be too late.

ii) Counter intelligence: Do not forget that your competitor is also trying to get information on you. You will have to ensure that he does not get any useful information on you or you can try to mislead him.

iii) Decision support system: What CI does is help you in taking a decision based on the data, which you have collected on your competitor.

c. Strategy formulation: No organization can formulate a strategy without CI. Kenichi Ohmae, the Japanese strategist had made a very pertinent point when he had said that 'If there is no competition, you do not require a strategy'.

In every business there are four types of players. They are,

Market leader, one number

Market challenger, one number

Market follower, 5 to 6 numbers

Market nichers, may be 200 and more

In order to put CI to use, you must know who you are? Then only competitive strategies can be put to use.

Please remember that the decisions are not made on information alone but on the options available to you. This results in strategy formulation.

The data, information and knowledge are on something, which has already happened. Any action based on that will be reactive. CI goes beyond that and that is why it is becoming a useful tool for the businesses. It serves two major purposes, that is,

• It is proactive, meaning; you can take action before the damage is done.

• It is futuristic, meaning; it does not talk about the past, but tells what will be the future scenario.

After all, we should all be concerned about the future because that is where we are going to spend the rest of our lives.

The development of CI

The development of CI is of recent origin. But, this is not true. It was always used in Wars right from the times of Shivaji- the great. He had a spy who is to infiltrate in Mughal army camps under different disguises.

He used to collect information on their numbers, availability of armory, their movements and many others. This was used by Shivaji in planning his offensive strategy. One can say that CI came from the Army.

However, as a management innovation, it came up over last 15 years or so. Benjamin Gilad, a Jew operating from Boston and Tel Aviv can be given the credit of being the Father of CI. He runs an Academy of Competitive Intelligence in Boston. His book on the subject 'Business Blind Spots' is a master piece. In this book, he gives illustrations of many companies how they ignore the happenings around them which can have great impact on them. The CEO believes that they have prepared a Business Plan and are monitoring it regularly. With this, every thing will be going fine for them. However, this does not always happen.

There is a world wide body which operates under the name of Society of Competitive Intelligence Professionals (SCIP). They have a collective membership of over 50,000 numbers in some 70 countries of the world. The authors were member of this organization for some time. This helped them in receiving literature, CD's and other material on the subject. More than that, it helped them in networking with CI professionals from other countries. They were approached by CI professionals from other countries from the members' directory and got consultancy assignments in these fields from companies who wanted to enter Indian markets.

Institutionalizing CI

CI cannot happen accidentally. Nor it can be left to chance. If ignored, it can prove dangerous to the survival of the company.

It is high time that the Indian government as well as other departments, corporates and every body starts thinking in terms of standardizing the requirements of CI. What is interesting is that CI does not require any capital investment. It is basically a change of the mindset. You could be at any level, in any functional area, you can keep your eyes and ears open and even any tid bits on the competitor could be useful to you.

You cannot stop the competition from entering the market. What you can do is through CI, you can defeat the competition with a clear margin.

ΟΟΟ

12 | Knowledge Management

Take a look at the following situations:

- A student as well as his/her parents would like to know what are the different courses available after passing the 10-12 th standard examination?

- A student after completing his graduation or post graduation would like to know what the different jobs available in the market are?

- An investor would like to know what the alternatives available for his surplus income are, what safety is available and what reasonable returns he can expect?

- A construction company would like to know what are the different projects which are coming up, when the tenders will be floated, what will be the last date and so on?

- You would like to go on vacation to the Eastern part of India and would like to know the different trains available to various destinations are and so on?

These are some of the examples, which will tell us that there is hardly anybody that is not looking for some or the other kind of information. The information is knowledge, which is communicated by others or obtained through studies and investigations. As Samuel Johnston, the seventeenth century philosopher had said, 'Knowledge is of two types. One which you possess individually, and the other, is to know where to get it'. If we are honest, we will soon realize that we have a limited knowledge of the first kind. However, there is no need to have any limitation of the second kind of knowledge.

Knowledge Management (KM) has emerged as an established discipline since 1995 with a body of university courses and both professional and academic journals dedicated to it. Many large companies have resources dedicated to KM, often as a part of 'Information Technology', 'Human Resource Management' or Business strategy departments. KM is a multi-billion dollar world-wide market.

Knowledge Management programs are typically tied to organizational objectives such as improved performance, competitive advantage, innovation, developmental processes, lessons learnt, for example between projects, and the general development of collaborative practices. Knowledge Management is frequently linked and related to what has become known as the learning organization, lifelong learning and continuous improvement. Knowledge Management may be distinguished from Organizational Learning by a greater focus on the management of knowledge as an asset and the development and cultivation of the channels through which knowledge, information and signal flow.

Knowledge Management

There is a broad range of thought on Knowledge Management with no unanimous definition. The approaches vary by author and school. Knowledge

Management may be viewed from each of the following perspectives:

Techno-centric: A focus on technology, ideally those that enhance knowledge sharing/growth.

Organizational: How does the organization need to be designed to facilitate knowledge processes? Which organizations work best with what processes?

Ecological: Seeing the interaction of people, identity, knowledge and environmental factors as a complex adaptive system.

In addition, as the discipline is maturing, there is an increasing presence of academic debates within epistemology emerging in both the theory and practice of knowledge management. British and Australian standards bodies both have produced documents that attempt to bound and scope the field, but these have received limited acceptance or awareness.

Knowledge Management has always existed in one form or another. Examples include on-the-job peer discussions, formal apprenticeship, discussion forums, corporate libraries, professional training and mentoring programs. However, with computers becoming more widespread in the second half of the 20th century, specific adaptations of technology such as knowledge bases, expert systems, and knowledge repositories have been introduced to further enhance the process.

The emergence of Knowledge Management has also generated new roles and responsibilities in organizations, an early example of which was the Chief Knowledge Officer (CKO). In recent years, Personal knowledge management (PKM) practice has arisen in which individuals apply KM practice to themselves, their roles and their career development.

Definition: KM is a system for managing the gathering, organizing, refining, analyzing and dissemination of knowledge in all form within and outside the organization.

Available forms: The knowledge is available in the following forms:

a) Print: It is available from the textbooks, magazines, newspapers, directories, reports prepared by various government and non-government organizations.

b) Digital: The Internet and the worldwide websites (www) have emerged today as the best sources of knowledge. There is hardly any subject on which knowledge does not exist. It is also marketed by various organizations in the form of CD/DVD's.

c) Human: Can technology replace human knowledge? Unlikely to be so. One can argue that this will be the best form of gathering knowledge. There are people from different spheres who can contribute to your knowledge.

Schools of thoughts in Knowledge Management

There are a variety of different schools of thought in Knowledge Management. These include:

• The intellectual capital movement proposed by Leif Edvinsson and Tom Stewart.

• A focus on collaboration including social planning concepts of community of practice, community consultation processes, public participation and a range of collaborative technologies. Much of this work originates from research by Etienne Wenger and the Lotus Institute (now absorbed into IBM

Research). Other prominent figures include Saint-Onge, McDermott and others.

- The use of social network analysis to understand interactions between people within organizations, both qualitatively and quantitatively, associated with Valdis Krebs, Stephen Borgatti, Robert L. Cross and others.

- A body of work derivative of information theory associated with Larry Prusak and Thomas H. Davenport and linked to the conversion of internalized tacit knowledge into explicit codified knowledge (SECI) allowing successful knowledge sharing as highlighted by Ikujiro Nonaka and Hirotaka Takeuchi. This is probably the dominant school of thought, as represented by publications and includes later developments by authors such as Probst, Von Krough & Malhotra amongst many others including Knowledge Asset Management.

- Management of tangibles & intangibles, living networks, co-creation and whole systems through value networks and value network analysis (Allee). This work also includes linkages and connections to theory associated with the Learning organization.

- Complexity approaches associated with David Snowden, Max Boisot, J C Spender and others. Variations of this include the use of narrative (Snowden, David M. Boje and others) as a form of fragmented knowledge.

- Systems thinking capacity based approach developed by Parent, Roy, & St-Jacques proposing a new knowledge management paradigm that views knowledge as a systemic, socially constructed, context-specific representation of reality. This is in sharp contrast to past approaches, focusing attention on the capacities that must be present in organizations and social systems as a precondition for knowledge transfer to occur.

Knowledge in this context is viewed not as an object to be transferred but as a by-product of interactions between individuals with varying capacities.

Two streams of knowledge management

There are so many persons who have come out with innovations on the subject of KM. However, credit must be given to the Swedish social scientist, Karl Sveiby for crystallizing the thoughts on the subject. It is not surprising that he is considered as the Father of Knowledge Management. He suggested that KM has two streams as described below:

Stream 1: This stream considers knowledge as an object or a product. This comprises of persons with background in computer programming. This is the IT-Track KM involved in the construction of information management systems. Today, several IT companies claim to operate in this area and offer products, which they call as KM products.

Stream 2: This stream considers knowledge as a process. This comprises of persons who are researchers and practitioners in the field of philosophy, sociology and/or management used for improving human individual skills and behavior. This is the People-Track KM for management of people.

Key concepts in Knowledge Management

Dimensions of knowledge

A key distinction made by the majority of knowledge management practitioners is distinction between tacit and explicit knowledge. The former is often subconscious, internalized, and the individual may or may not be aware of what he or she knows and how he or she accomplishes particular results. At the opposite end of the spectrum is conscious or explicit knowledge -- knowledge that the individual holds explicitly and consciously in mental focus, and may communicate to others. In the popular form of the distinction, tacit knowledge is something which is available after proper analysis, and explicit knowledge is available for everyone. See box.

a) On October 10, 2008 the stock markets crashed all across the world The Indian stock markets, both BSE & NSE tumbled, the former by as much as 1000 points. On Saturday, all the business papers gave the data on over 1000 scrips. This is the explicit data, which is available for everyone's knowledge. However, only those who are doing analysis of the same will be able to convert it in tacit knowledge. They would like to know the details on highs/lows of the various scrips, percentage gain/drop and such other details, which will help them in taking a decision on buy/sell.

b) A multi-product multi-market company has its sales data available. This is the explicit data. When it will be analyzed in terms of market growth, market share and profitability, it will be the tacit data, which will be used for formulating a strategy.

ii. Subjective and objective knowledge: Subjective knowledge will be focused on a specific domain while objective knowledge will offer wide choice.

iii. Know-what versus Know-how: To begin with, we will have to be clear what knowledge is required and later how it should be generated.

Steps in KM

Following steps will have to be performed.

- Knowledge gathering: We will have to identify all sources of information, primary as well as secondary for gathering of information. This will be a part of research methodology.

- Knowledge analysis: The knowledge compiled will require proper analysis with respect to the objectives.

- Knowledge diffusion: The knowledge gained will have to be made available to all and sundry.

- Knowledge exploitation: Ultimately, the importance of knowledge will be in its application. If it can be of use to improve the activities, then it will have meaning.

Requirement of KM

The KM must fulfill the following conditions:

- Futuristic: The data, information and knowledge would be from the past. However, KM will be looking ahead in the future.

- Proactive: The organizations will have to take proactive approach with the help of KM. The post mortem approach will not be useful.

- In usable form: It is quite likely that some knowledge will be too technical and complex. It is possible that a majority will not be able to understand the same. It will have to be simplified and put it in a usable form.

Managerial aspects of knowledge

a. What is knowledge? The knowledge needs will vary with respect to one's functional areas. Given below is a list of knowledge required by managers from different disciplines.

Marketing

- Product/Territory/End User/Middleman/Sales force contribution analysis
- Market share analysis
- Cost and profit analysis
- Marketing expenditure analysis
- Marketing effectiveness analysis
- Customer satisfaction measurement
- Attitudinal tracking
- Industry analysis and growth rate
- Competitor analysis
- Marketing environment analysis

Manufacturing

- Capacity utilization
- Down time
- Productivity
- Rejection rate
- Inventory control
- Vendor development
- Make or buy decisions

Research & development

- Product/process development
- Intellectual property rights
- Lead time
- Manpower budgets

Finance

- Financial performance analysis using financial ratios
- Capital structure (Debt/Equity)
- Budgeting and control
- Costing
- Debt servicing
- Tax planning
- Financial policies

Human resources

- Manpower data and analysis
- Cost of manpower (Direct/Indirect)
- Skills and motivational analysis
- Staff turnover, Recruitment & selection
- Planned training
- Leadership and succession planning

Strategic management

- Vision, mission and goals
- Strategic alliances
- Mergers & acquisitions
- Strategies

b. How is knowledge stored?: The knowledge compiled will have to be properly stored for the posterity as well as for the sue of all and sundry. This will be possible as follows;

- Data base management: DBM too has become a science. Starting from simple filing system, cardex system, the technology has revolutionized its storage. It has reduced the storage space dramatically and has increased the life of data stored substantially.

- Management information system: MIS emerged few years back as an important discipline in many organizations. Particularly for those, which could be described as multi-product, multi-market organizations, MIS provided the assistance to managers in decision-making.

c. How is knowledge managed?: Two alternatives are prominently used:

- Inter-organizational domains: Organizations are creating intranets for sharing of knowledge.

- Suppliers networks: This is done through internet and/or extranets

d. Sources of knowledge: There are two major sources that can be identified. They are:

- From within the organization: A periodic information audit can identify the necessary knowledge. It can identify the gaps which will help in deciding the efforts to fill them.

- From intelligence audit: Following alternatives can be put to use,

-Business environment: All aspects of business environment, both at macro and micro level can be studied.

Competitor environment: This will be part of competitor reconnaissance and understanding the strengths & weaknesses of all types of competitors.

Competitive environment: This will include the environment scanning continuously to identify factors which can affect the competitiveness of the organizations.

Problems in KM

It can be argued that KM also has few shortcomings. They can be identified as follows:

• Information overload: There is so much information available presently that a person gets confused. This is expressed in terms of Garbage. This requires precise definition of what knowledge is required so that the excess can be ignored.

• Lack of sharing: In a competitive environment, majority is afraid of sharing the knowledge available with them. This results in reinventing the wheel and duplication of efforts.

• Sorting and capturing tacit knowledge: The expertise to obtain the tacit knowledge from explicit knowledge is not available with all.

• Outdated and late: The knowledge can get outdated very fast. At the same time, if the knowledge is not available when needed urgently, then it will lose its importance.

• Wasteful expenditure: It is not necessary that KM require massive funds. Wasteful expenditures can be avoided if focus is clearly defined.

Use of technology in KM

Particularly in last 10 years or so, technology has played a major role in KM. Some of the major products, which have emerged in the market, are listed below:

• Internet, intranet and extranet
• Data mining and data warehousing
• Document management system
• Groupware

- Artificial intelligence
- Enterprise Resource Planning (ERP)
- Supply Chain Management (SCM)
- Customer Relationship Management (CRM0
- Benchmarking
- Measuring Intellectual Capital (MIC)

The principles & practices of management initially talked about resources of an organization in terms of 4M's. They were Material, Machinery, Manpower and Money. At that time, perhaps, they did not have an inkling that one more resource will emerge which will be more crucial for all organizations for survival and growth. We are referring to 1 I, and that was Information leading to Knowledge. If G.D. Birla was alive when the same dawned on us, he would have simply said that 'If you have knowledge with you, you are handsome, intelligent and you can sing well too' (He had said that about Rokda). All the managers are today called as knowledge workers and every one is keen to develop a knowledge organization.

What will be the role of knowledge in managing organizations? We will identify them as follows:

- Defining the core competency of the organization. This will help in chalking out the growth strategies.

- Creating a sustainable competitive advantage. Strategy is all about establishing a competitive advantage.

- Use of competitive intelligence to be forewarned and to develop a decision support system.

- Developing strategic options. As we have said before,

- decisions are not made on information, they are on options.

It is now for the individuals and organizations to decide how they will put KM to their advantage to succeed.

ooo

13 | Relationship Marketing

The great economist and the author of the book 'Wealth of Nations', Adam Smith had said that 'the primary business of any business is to remain in business'. Nobody will have a disagreement with him. However, he did not tell us how this is to be achieved?

While conducting the Entrepreneurship Development Programs (EDP'S), we invariably ask the question what inputs are needed to start a business. The answers invariably vary from capital, technology, machinery, raw materials and many others. The 'would be entrepreneurs', however, tend to forget the most important thing that is required to start and stay in business that is the customers! Not only we need customers to begin with, but, we want them to come back again and again for repeat purchases, that they should talk favorably about us and so on.

We believe that in any business organization, all disciplines like R &D, Production, Finance, HR and others are all equal. However, Marketing is the first amongst the equals! If the Marketing is ineffective, the role of other departments will be marginalized.

This simple principle has given rise to many innovations in the area of Marketing, which we plan to take up in this article.

I. Relationship Marketing

The marketing concepts have changed over the years from product, production, selling to the present one of customer orientation. However, most of the organizations still think that the consumers should adjust their needs & wants to the offering of the company. They seldom do analysis of their customers and offer special programs. The typical approach was, 'this is my product, take it or leave it'.

However, the scenario is changing mainly on account of the following factors:

- Marketing is becoming all pervasive. No organization can say that they do not need marketing.

- The consumers are becoming more demanding. Luckily for them, today, they have the backing of the law in the form Consumer Protection Act 1986.

- The competition is on the rise. It comes from brand, form, industry and from other generic products. It comes from domestic as well as from foreign players.

- The marketing environments are changing rapidly. Yesterday's target markets may not be tomorrow's target markets.

- The cost of marketing is on the rise. It has become imperative now to talk also in terms of Return on Marketing (ROM).

All these reasons have necessitated new paradigms.

Relationship marketing has the aim of building mutually

satisfying long-term relations with key partners. These will include consumers, customers, suppliers, channel members, shareholders and financial institutions. Marketers achieve this by promising and delivering high-quality products and services at fair prices to other parties overtime. Relationship marketing builds strong economic, technical and social ties among the parties. It cuts down on transaction costs and time. The ultimate outcome of relationship marketing is the building of a unique company asset called a marketing network. It consists of the company and its supporting stakeholders with whom it has built mutually profitable business relationships. It can now be said that now the competition is not between the companies but between marketing networks. Undoubtedly, those companies succeed who have built a better network. The operating principle is simple: Build an effective network of relationships with key stakeholders and profits will follow.

Relationship marketing differs from other forms of marketing in that it recognizes the long term value to the firm of keeping customers, as opposed to direct or "Intrusion" marketing, which focuses upon acquisition of new clients by targeting majority demographics based upon prospective client lists.

Development

Modern consumer marketing originated in the 1950s and 1960s as companies found it more profitable to sell relatively low-value products to masses of customers. Over the decades, attempts have been made to broaden the scope of marketing, relationship marketing being one of these attempts. Arguably, customer value has been greatly enriched by these contributions. It is said that the era of Mass Marketing is over. What we need today is Niche Marketing. This will cater to the specific needs & wants of all types of customers

The practice of relationship marketing has been facilitated by several generations of what is used today as customer relationship management, that allow tracking and analyzing of each customer's preferences, activities, tastes, likes, dislikes, and complaints. For example, an automobile manufacturer maintaining a database of when and how repeat customers buy their products, the options they choose, the way they finance the purchase etc., is in a powerful position to develop one-to-one marketing offers and product benefits.

Relationship marketing has also migrated back into direct mail, allowing marketers to take advantage of the technological capabilities of digital, toner-based printing presses to produce unique, personalized pieces for each recipient. Marketers can personalize documents by any information contained in their databases, including name, address, demographics, purchase history, and dozens (or even hundreds) of other variables. The result is a printed piece that (ideally) reflects the individual needs and preferences of each recipient, increasing the relevance of the piece and increasing the response rate. Personalized cheque books offered by the commercial banks is just one such example.

Scope

Relationship marketing has been strongly influenced by reengineering. According to (process) reengineering theory, organizations should be structured according to complete tasks and processes rather than functions. That is, cross-functional teams should be responsible for a whole process, from beginning to end, rather than having the work go from one functional department to another. Traditional marketing is said to use the functional department approach. The legacy of this can still be seen in the traditional four P's of the marketing mix in terms of

Product, Price. Place (Distribution) and Promotion. The marketing mix approach is too limited to provide a usable framework for assessing and developing customer relationships in many industries and should be replaced by the relationship marketing alternative model where the focus is on customers, relationships and interaction over time, rather than markets and products.

In contrast, relationship marketing is cross-functional marketing. It is organized around processes that involve all aspects of the organization. In fact, some commentators prefer to call relationship marketing "relationship management" in recognition of the fact that it involves much more than that which is normally included in marketing.

Some scholars believe that relationship marketing has the potential to forge a new synthesis between quality management, customer service management, and marketing. They see marketing and customer service as inseparable.

Relationship marketing involves the application of the marketing philosophy to all parts of the organization. Every employee is said to be a "part-time" marketer, meaning everyone is doing nothing but marketing."Marketing is not a function, it is a way of doing business . . . marketing has to be all pervasive, part of everyone's job description, from the receptionist to the board of directors."

Satisfaction

The basic premise in relationship marketing is generating customer satisfaction. Relationship marketing relies upon the communication and acquisition of consumer requirements solely from existing customers in a mutually beneficial exchange. With particular relevance to customer satisfaction the, relative price and quality of goods and services produced or sold through a company alongside customer service generally determine the amount of sales relative to that of competing companies.

Customer satisfaction is a state of mind of the customer when his expectations are fulfilled. A customer has expectations of different attributes when deciding to buy a product/service. He will have a certain priority given to each attribute. In comparison to different competing brands, he will allocate the weightages to different attributes. On this basis, he will make a purchase decision.

The customer satisfaction generally emerges based on the following factors:

- Easy availability of the products/services
- Consistency in quality
- Price competitiveness
- Excellent after-sales services

This results in developing loyal customers. However, this loyalty cannot be taken for granted. It has to be nurtured with the help of relationship marketing.

With the changing marketing scenario, more and more companies are investing in conducting customer satisfaction surveys. These can be used to develop a customer satisfaction index (CSI), let us say over a scale of 10. A periodic measurement can help in identifying areas of improvement.

Retention

It has been realized that, customer retention has become more important than customer satisfaction. A customer may be satisfied but may not come back for repeat purchase if he finds a better option.

A key principle of relationship marketing is the retention of customers through varying means and practices to ensure repeated trade from pre-existing customers by satisfying requirements above those of competing companies through a mutually beneficial relationship. This technique is now used as a means of counterbalancing new customers and opportunities with current and existing customers as a means of maximizing profit. Many companies in competing markets will redirect or allocate large amounts of resources or attention towards customer retention as in markets, with increasing competition, it may cost 5 times more to attract new customers than it would to retain current customers. It has been claimed that a 5% improvement in customer retention can cause an increase in profitability of between 25 and 85 percent (in terms of net present value) depending on the industry.

The increased profitability associated with customer retention efforts occurs because of several factors as listed below:

- The cost of acquisition occurs only at the beginning of a relationship, so the longer the relationship, the lower the amortized cost.

- Account maintenance costs decline as a percentage of total costs (or as a percentage of revenue).

- Long-term customers tend to be less inclined to switch, and also tend to be less price sensitive. This can result in stable unit sales volume and increases in Rupees-sales volume.

- Long-term customers may initiate free word of mouth promotions and referrals.

- Long-term customers are more likely to purchase ancillary products and high margin supplemental products.

- Customers that stay with you tend to be satisfied with the relationship and are less likely to switch to competitors, making it difficult for competitors to enter the market or gain market share.

- Regular customers tend to be less expensive to service because they are familiar with the process, require less "education", and are consistent in their order placement.

- Increased customer retention and loyalty makes the employees' jobs easier and more satisfying. In turn, happy employees feed back into better customer satisfaction in a virtuous circle.

Customer retention efforts involve considerations such as the following:

1. Customer valuation - how to value customers and categorize them according to their financial and strategic value so that companies can decide where to invest for deeper relationships and which relationships need to be served differently or even terminated.

2. Customer retention measurement - This is simply the percentage of customers at the beginning of the year that are still customers by the end of the year. In accordance with this statistic, an increase in retention rate from 80% to 90% is associated with a doubling of the average life of a customer relationship from 5 to 10 years. This ratio can be used to make comparisons between products, between market segments, and over time.

3. Determine reasons for defection - Look for the root causes, not mere symptoms. This involves probing for details when talking to former customers. Other

techniques include the analysis of customers' complaints and competitive benchmarking.

4. Implementation of a corrective plan - This could involve actions to improve employee practices, using benchmarking to determine best corrective practices, visible endorsement of top management, adjustments to the company's reward and recognition systems, and the use of "recovery teams" to eliminate the causes of defections.

Application

Relationship marketing and traditional (or transactional) marketing are not mutually exclusive and there is no need for a conflict between them. A relationship oriented marketer still has choices at the level of practice, according to the situation variables. Most firms blend the two approaches to match their portfolio of products and services. Virtually, all products have a service component to them and this service component has been getting larger in recent decades. What Theodore Levitt wrote in his classical article, 'The tangible Product'- every tangible product requires an intangible service, and every intangible service can have a tangible product!

Internal marketing

Relationship marketing also stresses what it calls internal marketing. This refers to using a marketing orientation within the organization itself. It is claimed that many of the relationship marketing attributes like collaboration, loyalty and trust determine what "internal customers" say and do. According to this theory, every employee, team, or department in the company is simultaneously a supplier and a customer of services and products. An employee obtains a service at a point in the value chain and then provides a service to another employee further along the value chain. If internal marketing is effective, every employee will both provide and receive exceptional service from and to other employees. It also helps employees understand the significance of their roles and how their roles relate to others'.

If implemented well, it can also encourage every employee to see the process in terms of the customer's perception of value added, and the organization's strategic mission. Further it is claimed that an effective internal marketing program is a prerequisite for effective external marketing efforts.

II. Delighting the Customers

So, it is more, much more than creating a successful transaction. It is about a relationship that is far stronger.

Top Ten Things about Delighting Customers:

Think of a time when you went 'Wow - that experience was something...'. It could have been a call centre, a store or at your doctor's receptionist. Sometimes, just sometimes, you get such memorable service you want more - and that place is special.

The very best places at Delighting Customers...

1. Have confidence

They have people who are at the top of their game because they have the right training and use it in an enlightened culture.

2. Have Fun

By encouraging fun with each other, their people have fun with their customers and build happy relationships. This builds for the future.

3. Do More

By 'going the extra mile', their people show they care - not just superficially - but truly care for their customers

4. Put Customers First

No distraction gets in the way of being there for the customer. Great places have people who, come what may, have their customer's needs first.

5. Empower Their People

In this way, their people are allowed to do anything that gets the very best outcome for their customers. They are encouraged to make sensible decisions to exceed the expectations of their customers.

6. Workaround Processes

They realize that whilst processes and systems are important, they are secondary to the needs of their customers.

7. Are Very Aware

They sense well. Meaning that they take in behaviors, words, moods and other signs to appreciate customer needs - in the moment; straight away, which strengthens the bond between them.

8. Follow through

They do what they say they will do. Promises are always kept and everyone understands that as a given.

9. Respond to Feedback

And as the people are aware, they also pick up signals and signs. Where change is necessary, they respond urgently. They understand accountability and nothing slips by.

10. Treat Their Own People Very Well

In such organizations, their people are always treated well and there is a culture of trust and honesty. No one is ever blamed, though lessons are learned and in a supportive and generative way. This is reflected in their work with customers

III. Partnership marketing (Back marketing)

Many organizations push their products & services down the throats of the customers without verifying whether it is meeting their requirements. See these examples:

- Banks give loans to the start-up companies without verifying the correct requirements. When the borrower unit becomes a defaulter, rather than help it, they start the legal proceedings to recover the loan. No wonder, the sickness, particularly in SME sector is on the rise.

- Insurance companies push their policies to the customers without understanding their short and long term financial needs.

In order to maintain a long term relationship with customers, a concept of partnership marketing came up. In earlier days, it was also called Back marketing. The principles are simple as   given below:

- Know the business of your client. Evaluate the environment, both macro and micro level. Identify their strengths & weaknesses.

- Compile data and spot opportunities for your client.

- Provide guidance on enterprise management to your client.

- Help the client to succeed

- Develop loyal customers

- Increase your own business

The box gives a very good illustration to explain this concept.

Mahindra & Mahindra Ltd. are automobile giants, manufacturing multi-utility vehicles and tractors mainly. These are their two SBU's respectively. The tractor division met to decide 'how they should be able to increase the sale of their tractors' whose end user is a farmer. They agreed that this will be possible only if the farmer makes more money, has more to spend on mechanization and so on. An elaborate plan was developed to help the farmers. It may sound funny, but, the company decided that for 32 years they were only selling the tractors to their customers which now they will cease to do. Instead, now they will provide total guidance to the farmer in better farm management. They developed the following strategies:

- They set up four model farms across the country and invited the farmers to visit them and obtain guidance in better farm management. The average land holding of the Indian farmer is meager 2.3 acres. The crucial question was how to get maximum yields from this limited land holding?

- The company provided guidance on selection of seeds, efficient use of lift irrigation, proper plant protection and avoiding use of harmful chemicals.

- Use of mechanization to improve efficiency.

- Proper grading of agricultural produce, proper preservation through pre-cooling and air-conditioned storage and attractive packaging.

- Perhaps the best help was offered in identifying and reaching domestic as well as overseas markets which will give the farmers more remunerative prices.

- Mahindra Finance Company offered them the working capital at reasonable rates.

It can be seen that no area was untouched which will

not be of help to the farmers. This ensured success for farmers. The strategy helped M &M to consolidate their market position and are today undisputed market leaders, not only in India but have aspirations to become the largest producers of tractors in the world. A very good example of partnership marketing! Other companies can emulate this example for their own benefit.

IV. Customer relationship Management (CRM)

Customer relationship management (CRM) is a term applied to processes implemented by a company to handle its contact with its customers. CRM invariably uses technology of software to support these processes, storing information on current and prospective customers. Information in the system can be accessed and entered by employees in different departments, such as sales, marketing, customer service, training, professional development, performance management, human resource development, and compensation. Details on any customer contacts can also be stored in the system. The rationale behind this approach is to improve services provided directly to customers and to use the information in the system for target marketing

While the term is generally used to refer to a software-based approach to handling customer relationships, most CRM software vendors stress that a successful CRM strategy requires a holistic approach. CRM initiatives often fail because implementation was limited to software installation without providing the appropriate motivations for employees to learn, provide input, and take full advantage of the information systems.

Overview

From the outside, customers interacting with a company perceive the business as a single entity, despite often interacting with a variety of employees in different roles and departments. CRM is a combination of policies, processes, and strategies implemented by a company that unify its customer interaction and provides a mechanism for tracking customer information.

CRM includes many aspects which relate directly to one another:

- Front office operations — Direct interaction with customers, e.g. face to face meetings, phone calls, e-mail, online services etc.

- Back office operations — Operations that ultimately affect the activities of the front office (e.g., billing, maintenance, planning, marketing, advertising, finance, manufacturing, etc.)

- Business relationships — Interaction with other companies and partners, such as suppliers/vendors and retail outlets/distributors, industry networks (lobbying groups, trade associations). This external network supports front and back office activities.

- Analysis — Key CRM data can be analyzed in order to plan target-marketing campaigns, conceive business strategies, and judge the success of CRM activities (e.g., market share, number and types of customers, revenue, profitability).

Types/Variations of CRM

There are several different approaches to CRM, with different software packages focusing on different aspects. In general, Campaign Management and Sales

Force Automation form the core of the system (with SFA being the most popular).

Operational CRM

Operational CRM provides support to "front office" business processes, e.g. to sales, marketing and service staff. Interactions with customers are generally stored in customers' contact histories, and staff can retrieve customer information as necessary.

The contact history provides staff members with immediate access to important information on the customer (products owned, prior support calls etc.), eliminating the need to individually obtain this information directly from the customer.

Operational CRM processes customer data for a variety of purposes:

- Managing Campaigns
- Enterprise Marketing Automation
- Sales Force Automation

Strategy

Several commercial CRM software packages are available, and they vary in their approach to CRM. However, as mentioned above, CRM is not just a technology but rather a comprehensive, customer-centric approach to an organization's philosophy of dealing with its customers. This includes policies and processes, front-of-house customer service, employee training, marketing, systems and information management. Hence, it is important that any CRM implementation considerations stretch beyond technology toward the broader organizational requirements.

The objectives of a CRM strategy must consider a company's specific situation and its customers' needs and expectations. Information gained through CRM initiatives can support the development of marketing strategy by developing the organization's knowledge in areas such as identifying customer segments, improving customer retention, improving product offerings (by better understanding customer needs), and by identifying the organization's most profitable customers.

Implementation Issues CRM strategies can vary in size, complexity, and scope. Some companies consider a CRM strategy only to focus on the management of a team of salespeople. However, other CRM strategies can cover customer interaction across the entire organization. Many commercial CRM software packages provide features that serve the sales, marketing, event management, project management, and finance industries.

While there are numerous reports of "failed" implementations of various types of CRM projects, these are often the result of unrealistic high expectations and exaggerated claims by CRM vendors.

Many of these "failures" are also related to data quality and availability. Data cleaning is a major issue. If a company's CRM strategy is to track life-cycle revenues, costs, margins, and interactions between individual customers, this must be reflected in all business processes. Data must be extracted from multiple sources (e.g., departmental/divisional databases such as sales, manufacturing, supply chain, logistics, finance, service etc.), which requires an integrated, comprehensive system in place with well-defined structures and high data quality. Data from other systems can be transferred to CRM systems using appropriate interfaces.

Because of the company-wide size and scope of many CRM implementations, significant pre-planning is essential for smooth roll-out. This pre-planning involves a technical evaluation of the data available and the technology employed in existing systems. This evaluation is critical to determine the level of effort needed to integrate this data.

Equally critical is the human aspect of the implementation. A successful implementation requires an understanding of the expectations and needs of the stakeholders involved. An executive sponsor should also be obtained to provide high-level management representation of the CRM project.

An effective tool for identifying technical and human factors before beginning a CRM project is a pre-implementation checklist. A checklist can help ensure any potential problems are identified early in the process. See box.

A senior business executive was a regular customer of a five star hotel in Chennai. Once while flying from his HQ to Chennai, he was horrified to find that his baggage was missing. All he had was his brief case carrying business papers. While checking, he explained his plight at the reception. No sooner he reached his room, a hotel attendant came with a package carrying a pair of under clothes, toiletries and other essentials.

He requested the guest to give his clothes which he was wearing for pressing which he brought back in 15 minutes. There was much more in store for the guest. He found a note saying that as he has a back trouble, a special hard bed has been offered in the room. The guest is diabetic. A note said that the room has anti-sugar sweeteners (Equal) for him. The hotel promised that they

---

will follow-up with the airlines to recover his baggage as early as possible. They kept the promise as his bag came by the evening flight intact. No wonder he is a satisfied and loyal customer of the hotel!

In this era of globalization and marketing warfare, relationship marketing, customer delight, back marketing and CRM could give an organization the much needed competitive edge. What is important is that these innovations do not require any capital cost. All it requires is a mindset which will consider consumer as king.

OOO

14 | Managing in Turbulent Times

Dr. P.C. Shejwalkar is a name to reckon in Pune in management education. He is also one of the very few persons who regularly sends us his feedback on our articles which appear in 'Sampada' of MCCIA. While commenting on our article thirteen in the last issue, he expressed a desire that we should write on the present bleak economic scene and how an individual as well as an organization should take steps, first to survive in this holocaust, and later manage to grow?

We are acceding to his request and are penning down our thoughts under the heading Managing in Turbulent Times. This title is not our original. In the late eighties, when the world was witnessing similar situation, the doyen of management education- Peter Drucker had come out with a book with this title. His opening remarks were very pertinent. He had said that, 'the world is going through a tough time. Let everyone realize, that these tough times are here to stay. This is on account of globalization, recession in several parts of the world, paucity of funds and many others. All organizations will have to gear themselves up to develop a mechanism to withstand it, forever'.

Needless to say, this is not a part of Management Innovation on which we are writing. However, the topic is so crucial at this juncture that it cannot be ignored. If the observations made by us are found useful by individuals as well as organizations, it will fulfill the aim of any management innovation, and that is, to bring improvements in the performance.

Few Happenings

Given below are the headlines which have appeared in the print media in last fifteen days or so.

- Tata Motors Ltd. announces another block closure and will work for only three days a week.

- Jet Airways will not renew the licenses of expat pilots.

- Bombay stock Market index at the lowest level in last three years. Real estate shares are the worst hit.

- The rate of inflation comes down to 6.6 per cent.

- Placement scene for the 2009 pass out batch looks precarious. Offers made by many companies are withdrawn.

- Real estate prices have crashed by more than 30%.

- Automobile manufacturers offering substantial discounts on their various models to increase sales.

- Much other similar depressing news.

This is not the picture in India alone. This is, perhaps, for the first time, a global scenario. In USA, the picture is even grim. Lehman Brothers, a 158 year old company has declared bankruptcy. Same has been the fate of Merrill Lynch. American Insurance Company (AIG) was baled out by the US Government. The automobile giants like General Motors, Ford and Chrysler have asked for a similar bale out package. Almost all major organizations have gone for massive manpower cut. Hewlett Packard (HP) announcing the layoff of 25,000 persons from one of their divisions.

What is interesting is that this downturn is not only to an Organization alone, but, on a larger scale, is affecting even the entire nation. Can you believe that even a country can declare itself bankrupt? That has exactly happened with Iceland which has declared bankruptcy. Pakistan is also on the edge and several other nations are in the queue.

Turbulent (adjective): Unruly, violent, uncontrolled, and riotous

As we can see, there are different meanings to the word. However, the word uncontrolled will be more apt for our discussion.

Major causes of turbulent times

There is a saying that when the problems come, they do not come as single soldiers but are in battalions. The present world wide turbulence is not caused by a single factor. It is the cascading effect of several factors. The major ones are given below:

- The American economy was buoyant from 2005-07 till the sub-prime crisis hit them badly. The home sales were on the rise. The housing finance companies wanted to show that this rise will continue forever. They started giving loans to home buyers without verifying their credentials and asking for margin money. The default rate started going up. The real estate prices crashed and all housing finance companies came in trouble.

- The USA has become a debtor's nation. More jobs were outsourced. First, it was in manufacturing area. Then came the services sector. The loss of American jobs to overseas workers rightfully created resentment.

- Several American companies, especially the financial institution did not follow the prudent norms needed in financial decisions. They started investing in projects which were not feasible, the top executives sanctioned huge bonuses to themselves and so on. When the money circulation came in difficulty, this created a panic situation.

- India is largely dependent on USA for its trade. With slowdown in American economy, the repercussions naturally were felt by the Indian companies. The worst hit was the IT & ITES sector.

For Indian IT companies, the bubble burst and they had to either layoff people or put them on the benches. This started a chain reaction. First, the real estate suffered because now the buying power started declining. The trend continued for the white goods industry.

- One major mistake which the CEO's make is that the good times will last forever. This does not happen. They ignore the signals which are given internally as well as from the external environments.

Theodore Levitt in his famous article Marketing Myopia had made a very pertinent statement. He had said that, 'there is nothing like a growth organization. What are available are growth opportunities which are provided by the marketing environments. The history of every growth organization shows a self deceiving cycle of bountiful expansion and undetected decay'.

Role of governments

When turbulence hits the economy, everyone looks

towards the government. Should it be the responsibility of the governments to bale them out? Particularly, when the poor performance of the organizations is their own doing? We do not think so. The organizations and the CEO's of the company must pay for their follies. But, this does not happen. The governments have to take a more benevolent stand in the larger interest of the nation and society. Particularly, they are more worried about the loss of jobs and rate of inflation which in most of the civilized societies is the major issue in the election year. Not so in India. Here the elections are fought most on non-issues and on caste considerations.

Given below are some of the measures which have been taken by the governments in USA and India:

- The US government has offered massive funds to the organization in the form of loans.

- In both USA and in India, the Repo Rates have been cut down. This is the rate of interest at which the banks borrow money from one another as well as from the Reserve Bank of India (RBI). In other words, the cost of finance has been reduced. Second fiscal measure which was taken by the governments is to reduce the Cash reserve Ratio (CRR). With this, more money is available in the market to the industry & business. This money is being used for meeting their working capital needs and there by giving a boost to the economy.

- The Government of India (GOI) has reduced the excise duty on all types of products. This should result in the reduction of prices and should increase the consumption. The manufacturers are supposed to pass on this advantage to the consumers to stimulate the demand.

- Unfortunately, this always does not happen and many unscrupulous manufacturers use this to increase their profitability. One such major illustration is that of the oil industry. When the prices of a barrel of crude oil touched the level of USD147 per barrel, the prices of petroleum products were increased substantially. However, when the prices of a barrel of crude oil have come below USD 50, the petroleum companies are not passing on the advantage to the consumers. They are involved in profiteering. We feel that the manufacturers should behave in a more responsible manner if they have to earn the respect of their consumers.

- The governments can announce reduction in duties & taxes, rate of income tax, offer incentives to set up new businesses and many others. We feel that this is the power which is available in the hands of all the governments to come up with appropriate fiscal policies to boost the economy.

It also must be remembered that when the economy of the country goes through bad times; it also affects the revenue of the governments. The collection of duties & taxes can decline. Under such circumstances, the governments will also have to prune down their budgets, cut on wasteful expenditures and so on so forth. Unfortunately this does not happen. India's Prime Minister Dr. Manmohan Singh had to request his ministerial colleagues to cut down on their foreign visits unless it is a must. However, the ministers and their staff have ignored this plea and as has been reported in media, their foreign binges continue.

Strategies for individuals

Sant Kabir in one of his poems (Doha) had said that ' Dukh main sumiran sab kare, sukh main kare na koi, jo sukh main sumiran kare, to dukh kahe ko hoye (when bad times come, we all start praying to the God, but, if we have been praying the God in good times too, there will never be bad times). This is exactly what happens with individuals. Given below are some of the things that can happen during the turbulent times.

- An individual can lose his/her job and regular earning which comes with it.

- A person may have to take a cut in the salary.

- The investments made may decline and the assured return on investments may not be forthcoming. If this is happening with increasing rate of inflation, it becomes a double problem for individuals.

- There are certain costs like school fees, daily living expenses and some others which cannot be curtailed.

What should be done under such circumstances? We would suggest the following:

- To begin with do proper budgeting of the income & expenditure. Prepare a cash flow statement at least for next three months regularly. This can take into anticipation the likely expenses which will be due in this period like premium for life insurance, tuition fees of the children and such other 'must to be paid' expenses.

- Cut down on expenses which can be avoided. For example, eating in fancy restaurants, seeing the movies in multiplexes, purchase of costly white goods, a trip to a tourist destination and so on.

- Look for investment opportunities which are safe and at the same time will give higher returns. One must understand the difference between 'expenses' and 'investments'.

- While the former needs to be reduced, the same treatment may not be given to the latter. For example, the Stock Market has reached a bottom level. At this level, it is possible to acquire stocks of blue chip companies who have strong fundamentals and in normal times offer attractive returns. Patience will be required at this stage on the part of the investor. Done prudently, it can result in a 'Kill' for them.

- If possible, look for additional sources of income. A part time job if available can be tried.

- Increased the savings for a rainy day.

Strategies for organizations

The companies should also view 'turbulent' times from two lenses - expenditures and investment. They should cut expenditures where necessary to impact short term profitability; this could range across all items of the P&L statement. Companies should maintain a strict eye on ROI and spend only where necessary. Discretionary spending should be scrutinized carefully.

It has become worldwide phenomena that during turbulent times, most of the organizations go for downsizing. We have different views on the subject. See box.

We are reading every day the news item on laying off of employees by all types of organizations. How does this affect the morale of them as well as those who still have jobs in their hands? Most of the persons report to the office in the morning with a fear whether it is their turn to get the 'pink slip'. We will be blunt in our observations that laying off people is an admission of defeat on the part of the CEO. He/she can explore many other options before such a drastic step is taken resulting in chaos at every level.

We will draw some similes here. It takes 20 years to have a full grown tree. It takes only 20 minutes to cut the tree with the help of modern machinery.

It takes 20 years to have an effective manager. It takes less than 20 seconds to tell him/her that 'you are fired'. When the normalcy returns, how are you going to replace the person who had a substantial experience and would prove beneficial to the organization in future?

We find it funny when reputed management consultancy companies approach organizations to offer consultancy in 'downsizing'. We believe that you do not require a consultant to tell you this and charge a fat fee. Yes, you can use a consultant who will give you guidance in doubling the turnover in four years without losing a single job in turbulent times. Where are such consultants?

We would be more specific and offer our suggestions for different functional areas.

Marketing

It is said that when the going gets tough, the tough get going. Marketing people will have to demonstrate this toughness. Given below are some of the strategies they can be put to use:

- Do a thorough analysis of sales performance over the years and identify the target markets who offer best potential. The power of analytics can be put to use in developing a winning strategy.

- When the recession strikes, the consumption does not become zero. It only reduces by certain percentage as compared to the earlier years. Under the circumstances, the organization will have to increase its marketing efforts to retain its market share in this reduced market. The number of visits will have to be increased, relationship marketing will have to be put to use.

- The organization can go for increase usage by existing customers, new applications and new geographical markets.

- Instead of lowering the prices, go for more value addition services. Put the 'back marketing' to use to help the customers to succeed.

- Put a strict control on finished goods inventories, receivables and others.

- Improve the effectiveness of sales force, dealers and marketing communication. If possible, avoid costly media, reduce frequency, measure the effectiveness regularly to come out with course correction actions.

- The lean time can be put to use in training of marketing persons to make them improve their selling skills.

- This is the time when overseas markets can be explored. As the recession could be in different stages in different countries, it may offer a good potential. In order to penetrate these markets, the principle of marginal costing could also be put to use.

- Trying to generate more revenue through offering annual maintenance contracts and genuine spares.

A general belief is that during turbulent times, the first axe always falls on marketing expenses. We feel that this is not the right approach. On the contrary, the marketing efforts need to be doubled. At the same time ensuring that every rupee spent on marketing is bringing that Return on Marketing (ROM)

Manufacturing

With the reduction in demand, the loading of the production facilities will also go down. Under the circumstances, following possibilities can be tried:

- Reduction in number of shifts in tune with market demands.

- Offering facilities which are not fully utilized for use to other manufacturers and there by generation of revenue.

- An energy audit at this stage can help in reducing the energy bills.

- An evaluation in 'Make or Buy' decisions to cut down on costs.

- Improving maintenance and thereby reducing the 'down time'.

- Improving quality through such tools like 6-Sigma, TQM , Kaizen and others

Purchase

The purchase department too can play a major role. Particularly for industrial products, the raw materials and other consumables take a major share in the costs. Following possibilities can be explored:

- Negotiating lower prices without compromising on quality.

- Looking for vendors, not only in India, but through global outsourcing where the costs can be reduced.

- Maintaining appropriate inventory levels which will reduce the costs but at the same time should not result in lost opportunities.

- Negotiating for payment terms which can offer a

longer credit period, volume or off season discounts and others.

- Identifying transportation alternatives where by the costs can be reduced.

Finance

In turbulent times, companies which shore up their financials - reduce inventories, debt level, improve accounts receivables and accounts payables, increase cash, and place them in a better position to scoop up assets or make investments at attractive prices and potentially with attractive returns. Companies should put greater effort to cleaning up their balance sheet and identifying investment opportunities. Some possibilities are given below:

- An overall cost cutting across the divisions and functional areas.
- Taking a salary cut. This will be preferred by employees any day rather than lose the job. See box.

Lee Iacocca was a legendary CEO from USA. He was the President of Ford Motor Company when he had difference with his boss and was sacked. He was in limbo for some time before he was called to turn around the sick Chrysler Corporation. He did a thorough study of the expenses and found that if the workers agree to the wages of USD 12 per hour, it is possible to turn around the company. The workers union was demanding a wage of USD 18 per hour. He called the Union leader and told him bluntly, that at USD12 per hour, they have a job. However, if they insist on USD 18 per hour, they will all be unemployed. Iacocca gave them 24 hours to think and come back to him. The Union Leaders came back within one hour and agreed to work for the rate suggested by him. The turnaround of Chrysler is now part of the legend in the business histories worldwide.

Human resources division (HRD)

We feel that this department has a major role to play during the turbulent time. The most important thing for them is to keep the morale high at all times. The bad news from the industry world wide will be filtering in and it will be a difficult task to mange the above. We would suggest the following action on the part of this division:

- Improve the corporate communication. At this juncture, the rumors spread very fast which reduces the productivity as well as the morale.

- Maintain transparency and explain the reasons if the company has to lay off people. Help them in finding other jobs. They may take the help of a psychiatrist, if needed.

- Offer training programs to keep them busy and to improve their skills and effectiveness.

- Avoid replacements of people quitting, retiring and any other causes. This may entail working of longer hours for the remaining few.

Leadership

We have been repeatedly saying that management philosophy is very clear. It states that the 'failure is always at the top'. It is expected from the CEO to anticipate the changes taking place in the environments. He/she should be prepared for the same with contingency measures. However, if the worst happens on which he/she has no control, then his mettle will be tested. If he can steer the company during turbulent times, he will be heralded as a leader. Otherwise, he will be termed as failure.

We read about several organizations where the CEO's were sacked for the poor performance of their organizations. However, what amuses us, particularly, from American companies, is when these failed CEO's are given fat severance salaries. Some names which come to our mind immediately are that of Carly Fiorina (Hewlett & Packard), Prince (Citibank) etc

Leadership should galvanize their workforce to drive harder. Leader should support their employees because naturally morale is low. Strong leadership is critical in turbulent times. Tough times do not last long, only the tough people do is a popular saying. At the same time, the CEO cannot just call it a universal phenomena and does not even try. He/she will have to garner all resources available at his disposal and put them to the best use. And, the most important resource will be the people. If he can develop the team spirit, any amount of turbulence can be overcome collectively.

OOO

15 | Social Innovation

We are proud to admit that JRD Tata is one of our role models. In a letter written to a school teacher in Jamshedpur, JRD gave a list of his guiding principles. This has become a mission statement for many individuals and organizations. One of the principles he had enumerated is given below:

No success or achievement in material terms is worthwhile unless it serves the needs or interest of the country and its people and is achieved by fair and honest means.

Mind well, JRD had written this letter sometime in late seventies when terms like Corporate Social Responsibility (CSR) had not become a topic for seminars in five star hotels and taken pages in the annual reports of the companies! It had also not become a law under section 49 of Corporate Governance. This is perhaps a first introduction to the subject of Social Innovation by an industry stalwart.

Social Innovation is the topic of this article. Innovation is not limited to entrepreneurs or large corporations. Today, social innovation which aspires to serve under represented segments of the market is coming mainstream. Mohammad Yunis who won the Nobel Prize for Grameen bank is perhaps the most well known example of an idea that changed the face of lending forever. What is social innovation? What role can it play in society? Let's explore further through the following dimensions:

Social Aspects of Marketing

The exchange process between organizations and target customers aiming at improving the plight of the latter has been termed as Social Marketing. It can be elaborated under three headings.

Social marketing: This will ensure that the sellers will offer the best products & services to the customers, that they will not create artificial shortages, under weigh, overcharge and deny the after sales services. They will respect the rights of the buyers and will continuously aim at generating customer satisfaction.

Societal marketing: This will include all those activities which will aim at creating resources for the benefit of the common man. Depending on the choice of the organizations, they can take up any activity. This may include building shelters for bus stops, maintenance of gardens, providing drinking water and many others. This input is today being termed as CSR. Tata group of companies are in the forefront of this activity. See box.

Social cause marketing: Our country has many problems. They may include issues like family planning, drug addiction, HIV aids, pollution, deforestation and many others. Individuals and organizations can take up any of these problems and work towards minimization of the same. This could be done through media campaigns to create awareness and prompting people to be sensitive on them.

It is amazing to put on record what Tata's have done for this nation. A partial list is given below:

- Setting of Indian Institute of Science in Bangalore
- Setting up of Tata Institute of Social Science (TISS) and Tata Institute of Fundamental Research (TIFR) in Mumbai
- Setting up of Tata Cancer Research Hospital in Mumbai
- The modern city of Jamshedpur
- Tata Management Training Centre in Pune
- Many others

Social Innovation Explained

Social innovation refers to new strategies, concepts, ideas and organizations that meet social needs of all kinds - from working conditions and education to community development and health - and that extend and strengthen civil society.

Over the years, the term has developed several overlapping meanings. It can be used to refer to social processes of innovation, such as open source methods and techniques. Alternatively it refers to innovations which have a social purpose - like micro credit or distance learning. The concept can also be related to social entrepreneurship (entrepreneurship isn't always or even usually innovative, but it can be a means of innovation) and it also overlaps with innovation in public policy and governance.

Social innovation can take place within government, within companies, or within the non-profit sector (also known as the third sector), but is increasingly seen to happen most effectively in the space between the three sectors. The Non Government Organizations (NGO's) are doing a yeoman service across the country in many areas. The self less and devoted leadership is seen only in this area.

History

Social innovation was discussed in the writings of Peter Drucker and Michael Young (founder of the Open University and dozens of other organizations) in the 1960s. It also appeared in the work of French writers in the 1970s, for example Pierre Rosanvallon, Jacques Fournier, and Jacques Attali.

However, the themes and concepts in social innovation have existed long before that. Benjamin Franklin, for example, talked about social innovation in terms of small modifications within the social organization of communities that could help to solve everyday problems. Many radical 19th century reformers like Robert Owen, founder of the cooperative movement, promoted innovation in the social field and all of the great sociologists including Karl Marx, Max Weber and Émile Durkheim focused much of their attention to broader processes of social change. However, more detailed theories of social innovation only became prominent in the 20th century.

Joseph Schumpeter, for example, addressed the process of innovation more directly with his theories of creative destruction and his definition of entrepreneurs as people who combined existing elements in new ways. In the 1980s and after, writers on technological change increasingly addressed the importance of social factors in affecting technology diffusion.

The idea of social innovation has become much more prominent with ongoing research, blogs and websites (such as the social innovation exchange), and a proliferation of organizations working on the boundaries of research and practical action. Several currents have converged in this area, including:

New thinking about innovation in public services, pioneered particularly in some of the Scandinavian and Asian countries. Governments are increasingly recognizing that innovation isn't just about hardware: it is just as much about prisons and healthcare, schooling and democracy. The successful experiments conducted by Kiran Bedi in Tihar Jail are one such example.

• Growing interest in social entrepreneurship.

• Business, which is increasingly interested in innovation in services.

• New methods of innovation inspired by the open source field.

• Linking social innovation to theory and research in complex adaptive systems to understand its dynamics.

• Collaborative approaches to social innovation, particularly in the public sector.

History of Social Innovation and territorial development

A recent overview of the field highlighted the growing interest of public policy makers in supporting social innovation in these different sectors, notably in the UK, Australia, China and Denmark. A focus of much recent work has been on how innovations spread and on what makes some localities particularly innovative. India has not been lagging behind as will be seen by the illustrations given elsewhere.

There is another extensive literature on social innovation in relation to territorial (or regional) development, which covers: first, innovation in the social economy, i.e. strategies for satisfaction of human needs; and second, innovation in the sense of transforming and/or sustaining social relations, especially the governance relations at the regional and local level. A combination of both the modes provides a comprehensive approach to innovation in social and economic dynamics within territories.

In Europe, from the late 1980s, research on social innovation from a territorial perspective was initiated by Jean-Louis Laville and Frank Moulaert and has been going on since then. In Canada CRISES initiated this type of research. The first large scale research project to work on territorial innovation analysis was SINGOCOM Social Innovation, Governance, and Community Building a European Commission Framework 5 project (2002-2004), that offered wide ranging discussions on Alternative Models for Local Innovation (ALMOLIN).

India Today (July 07, 2008) came out with a special issue in their four part Spirit of India on innovators from different parts of India. They titled this as Pioneers of Change. We would urge the readers to revisit these pages and see for themselves how people from rural areas, mostly uneducated, are capable of coming out with innovations which will be of great help to the society.

These men and women believe in their best lives. They do not believe in the hypothetical of 'could', 'would' or 'should'. They do not wait for the world to help them but commit their energies to doing what they can do themselves. Some set up organizations which have outlived them; others are at the cutting edge of transforming India through scientific innovation and social revolution. Some work for sheer altruism, others for profit.

They are the living embodiments of John F. Kennedy's famous words: they did not ask what the country could do for them, but, asked and answered the question what they could do for the country.

Muhammad Yunus

As a social innovator, mention will have to be made of this person. The Bangladeshi economist and founder of the Grameen Bank, an institution that provides micro credit (small loans to poor people possessing no collateral) to help its clients establish creditworthiness and financial self-sufficiency. In 2006, Yunus and Grameen received the Nobel Prize for Peace.

After teaching economics at Chittagong University from 1961 to 1965, Yunus won a Fulbright scholarship. He studied and taught at Vanderbilt University from 1965 to 1972, earning a Ph.D. in economics in 1969. He returned to Chittagong University as head of the economics department in 1972 and began studying the economic aspects of poverty in 1974 as famine swept through Bangladesh. Yunus even asked students to assist farmers in the fields, but he concluded that agricultural training alone would not benefit the large population of landless poor who had no assets. What the poor needed, he believed, was access to money that would help them build small businesses; traditional moneylenders charged usurious interest. In 1976 Yunus began a program of "micro" loans, a credit system designed to meet the needs of the poor in Bangladesh. Borrowers, whose loans may be little more than IR 1000/-, join lending groups. Support from group members (in addition to peer pressure) coaxes borrowers to repay their loans. The Bangladesh government made the Grameen Bank Project an independent bank in 1983.

The Grameen model concept of Yunus of 'micro credit' has caught on many parts of the world including India. There are close to 100 finance companies who are offering this help to entrepreneurs, mostly in rural areas.

We are offering below few examples of social innovation that have come to notice. These are the common people, in different age groups and gender, who are neither highly educated nor rich but are fired with a passion to contribute their mite to the society. These illustrations should inspire others and make them think 'If they can do it, why can't I?'

- Anita Ahuja (48) (Founder Conserve): She runs a project in Delhi, an NGO that creates accessories by recycling waste material. There are more than 100,000 rag pickers, of whom 40,000 are women. She makes sure waste doesn't go waste and re-uses it to create things of beauty. Her main aim is to ensure that every rag picker gets a share of a monthly salary.

- Mohd Islam Khan (70) from Firozabad became the first glass bangle manufacturer to adopt an energy efficient furnace developed by Tata Energy research Institute (TERI) and SDC in 2000. The temperature is nearly 75 degree Celsius near the furnace, the surface temperature being around 300 degrees Celsius. Heedless of the heat, men armed with steel rods, the tips glowing, walk to and fro thrusting the ends into the furnace.

- M. J. Joseph Appachan (50) from Kerala where there are close to 16 crore palm trees. There is an acute shortage of traditional coconut climbers and other manual labourers related to this age old profession. This small scale farmer and a high school dropout with the brain of a techie has invented a coconut tree climbing device which can be sued by anyone to climb a tree to pluck nuts, tap the basic ingredient of toddy, the indigenous liquor or spray insecticides.

- Kambel Chulai (69) from Meghalaya developed a modern eco-friendly crematorium which can be used anywhere as it runs on firewood. Instead of traditional crematorium using wood costs Rs.5000/-, this technique will need Rs.200/- worth of wood to cremate a body.

- Raghava Gowda (54) from Karnataka has developed a milking machine which will empower small farmers. There are close to 200 million cows in India, a majority owned by marginal farmers. This equipment will help them in improving their productivity and earnings.

- H. Harish Hande (40) is a B.Tech from IIT Kharagpur and pursuing a PhD in sustainable energy. Instead of taking a cushy corporate job, he decided to venture on his own. His project Selco provides customized solar lighting solutions. It is sad that solar energy, which is absolutely free, is only 0.5% of the total energy produced in India. The solution to poverty lies in sustainable energy.

- Mujeeb Khan (33) hasn't been able to walk since the age of two because of polio. Nearly, 600 polio cases were registered in India last year. He has developed designs for cars so that physically disabled person can drive.

- Madan Lal Kumavat (41) improvised time saving Thresher with attachments which adapts to different grains. India's total food grain production is close to 230 million tonne. This gadget will be of great boon to the farmers at a low cost.

- Arvind Patel (54) used the principle of evaporation in

developing a natural water cooler and a refrigerator that keeps vegetables fresh for long. The water cooler cools water to 23 degrees Celsius when the outside temperature is 44 degrees. 250 units of Patel's water cooler have been sold by the Gujarat Energy Development Agency (GEDA).

- Mansukhbhai Patel (54) dropped out of school in class XII. However, he came out with a design of an updated cotton stripper machine and it transformed him into a successful innovator. The machine was perfected by 1998 is now being used by 100 cotton ginning & pressing mills across the country.

- S. Rajagopalan (60) set up Technology Information Design Endeavour or TIDE comprising of 20 professionals at Bangalore wholeft their comfortable jobs to develop technology to the grass root levels. 74% of rural Indian households use firewood as cooking fuel. This results in deforestation. TIDE has developed over 100 technologies for the use of rural population.

- P. Mukundan (60) a Chennai based innovator developed in 2002 an ingeniously simple stove burner that cuts kerosene costs by 27% His target was the lakhs of people who cannot afford LPG.

- Institute of Kidney Diseases and Research Centre at Ahmadabad has done the highest number of of kidney transplants in the country. Crossing the 200 number, the centre has created an elaborate awareness program, building an effective network of donors and recipients. A traditional kidney transplant costs a minimum of Rs.1.5 lakhs. However, this institute has developed the technique of cadaver kidney transplant which costs only around Rs.10,000/-

- Harsha Moily (36) left a good job to work in India's villages. He set up a Rs. 1.45 crore microfinance firm which now has close to 27000 customers. The market is out there in the rural land, where the real India lives and works.

- R Shanmugham (52) near Coimbatore set up the first local body in the country to build its own 350 MW windmill, the first to have a community water supply scheme, the first to install a biomass gasifier to generate power. 40% of the population in India still does not have any electricity. Such successful ventures will encourage others to be self sufficient in energy.

These are just few of the examples of social innovation in India. What is important is that a majority is targeting the large rural population which over the years was completely ignored. It is also equally creditable that a reputed magazine like India Today took a note of their efforts and brought these common people in limelight.

At the same time, it must not be forgotten that there are many unsung heroes, who too have bright innovative ideas who are waiting to be discovered.

Areas in which social innovations needed

We did a small exercise to find out the concerns of common Punekars. A big list emerged where innovation is badly needed. We invite the readers to come out with suggestions what can be done to overcome these problems.

1. Poor conditions of roads

2. Frequent power interruptions

3. Traffic indiscipline

4. Increase in road accidents

5. Spitting habits

6. Garbage disposal

7. Rise in slums

8. People urinating on roads

9. Hoardings menace

10. Corruption at all levels

Dr. APJ Abdul Kalam has developed a vision for India for 2020. He has identified ten areas where he feels that Social Innovation will have to play its role. See box.

List of areas where social innovation is needed for India of 2020

1. A nation where the rural and urban divide is reduced to a very thin line.

2. A nation where there is equitable distribution of and adequate access and quality of water.

3. A nation where agriculture, industry and service sector work together in symphony.

4. A nation where education within a value system is not denied to any meritorious candidate because of societal and economic discrimination.

5. A nation which is the best destination for the most talented scholars, scientists and investors.

6. A nation where the best of healthcare is available to all.

7. A nation where governance is responsive, transparent and free of corruption.

8. A nation where poverty has been totally eradicated, illiteracy removed and crimes against women and

---

children are absent.

9. A nation that is prosperous, healthy, secure, peaceful and happy, on a sustainable growth path.

10. A nation that is one of the best places to live in and is proud of its leaders from all walks of life.

Social Innovation Ecosystem

In the above half of the article, we have reviewed the history of social innovation, recognized some people who are rendering yeoman service to the society through different social vehicles, and also prepared a list of areas that desperately need our attention.

To tackle social innovation, we have to design a social innovation ecosystem that supports the ideation – idea generation to innovation – product or service process.

Idea generation: Social innovations target large problems such as public health, care for the needy, education etc. Typically, there is no dearth of ideas to tackle, but it's important that idea generation focus on defining some boundaries or constraints to the idea rather than attempt to 'boil the proverbial ocean'. For e.g. Increase access of technology to all school children may be a very lofty goal versus providing one laptop to all school children above the age of 10 years (Google 'OLTP' (One laptop per child) initiative for some additional reading). Most ideas are constrained by the resources that can be allocated to them, and with social innovation concepts, it's easy to get carried away. Rather, the focus during this stage for the social entrepreneur should be to brainstorm on themes of interest but also tighten them so that they can be scoped out in common measures such as cost, time, revenue etc. It's always important though to measure the ideas based on their 'impact'. The goal should be to serve large underserved parts of the population that may be neglected by the more mainstream products. The list of social entrepreneurs offers ample evidence of such impactful projects.

Collaboration and project management: Social innovations require a robust ecosystem to succeed. Corporations can be roped in to help. For example, consultants from prestigious firms such as McKinsey often offer their time pro-bono to social projects. Local governments as well as the public can be invited to assist in social endeavors. Often social participation can carry benefits such as tax savings or generate good press for a company. For e.g. several companies act as sponsors of blood drives or eye clinics for the poor.

Finance presents a big bottleneck to social endeavors, and it's important for the principals to approach a social project with the same attention to detail as they would if they were working on a typical for profit venture. In a survey of the largest philanthropists, most preferred to distribute money to social ventures through their own foundations or trusts because they believe they can scrutinize every penny that passes through their fingers.

The goal here is to not necessarily focus on profit, but to ensure that all the necessary due diligence such as finance, operations, marketing, selling, people strategy – the building blocks of any successful enterprise have been studied properly. Since financiers are key collaborators in social ventures, if entrepreneurs prepare themselves to present their projects through the same filters financiers normally apply, they will increase their chances of raising money.

Collaboration with for profit corporations may also offer avenues for such corporations to make money while supporting social ventures. Social projects should always explore such alternatives. For e.g. a project conducted in a university in United States focused on creating a simple device that will sit on a kitchen table and record the electricity being consumed by household appliances. This was targeted at low income households so that they could curb their electricity usage. Now this device is being promoted by some utilities companies for energy conservation during peak load times. This has benefited the project by garnering it much needed funding.

In conclusion, social innovation must focus on large impact projects with broad social breadth. The attempt must be to bridge any divides that exist between mainstream and underserved segments with products or services that help do so. Lastly, social entrepreneurs should apply the same rigor to the ideation to innovation cycle they would if they were launching for profit more mainstream innovations.

Some food for thought as we sign out: A quote from the new President of the United States (words echoed by Mahatma Gandhi as well) 'You must be the change you wish to see in this world'.

○○○

16 | MBO, Metrics and Balance Score Card

The discipline of management is focused on the achievement of certain goals, so it should come as no surprise that the creation of tangible and measurable goals and objectives and scorecards to measure and monitor progress should follow. The science and the art of articulating the above has gone through a lot of change, and is adaptive in nature. Goals and objectives that are important today may not be so in the future as the demands on business change constantly. Why should management define objectives? (See box) How should it track progress against those objectives? What are scorecards or metrics? How should we design them? What are some of the best practices in this area? We shall explore these topics in this article.

Famous scientist, Albert Einstein is one of our favorites. There are so many anecdotes which are quoted on his name. This one shows the importance on what we are going to write.

Einstein was a German Jew who migrated to USA when Adolph Hitler started the persecution of Jews. Einstein visited his native country after the World War II got over. He was traveling on a train when a ticket checker accosted him. Absent minded professor as he was, he could not locate the ticket. He was absolutely sure that he had bought the ticket. Luckily for him, the ticket checker recognized him and said that,' of course, you are the famous scientist Albert Einstein. I have seen your photograph in the morning paper. I know that you will never travel without the ticket. Hence, as and when you locate it, kindly deposit it with the nearest railway station for our records'.

Einstein replied mischievously, 'My dear fellow, the problem is not where my ticket is? The problem is where am I going'?

The moral of the story: Unless you know where you are going, any road will take you there.

Introduction: Objectives are the filters that allow us to define our actions. If we draw upon the analogy of a traveler planning a journey to a certain destination, then we would characterize the destination as the objective, and once we have embarked on the journey, we will study our progress by measuring common metrics such as time elapsed or distance covered. Similarly, in business, organizations need to establish clear objectives to drive clear measurable actions. Although one can't call this as a management innovation in the classical sense as one would some of the others we have discussed in our previous articles, the art and the science of setting objectives acquired greater mindshare and a better definition when Peter Drucker coined the phrase 'Management by Objectives' in his book 'The Practice of Management' in 1954.

Core Concepts: (Source: Adopted from 1000 ventures. com) Management by objectives (MBO) is a systematic and organized approach that allows management to focus on achievable goals and to attain the best possible results from available resources. It aims to increase organizational performance by aligning goals and subordinate objectives throughout the organization. Ideally, employees get strong input to identify their objectives, time lines for completion, etc. MBO includes ongoing tracking and feedback in the process to reach objectives.

Peter Drucker instructed managers to avoid an 'activity trap' under which managers focused on the work and not on the results. In MBO, the result is the key area of focus. He encouraged managers to set objectives and then break them down into set of specific goals or results. It starts with a top down vision where the top brass in an organization outlines a vision and a set of goals and objectives. These translate into a set of goals and actions for all employees in the organization such that their deliverables and actions line up with the overall goals and objectives of the organization. Once these have been established, the company sets and communicates a clear set of guidelines (metrics and scorecards) for measuring the performance against those goals.

The following chart provides an illustration of the MBO cycle:

Review organizational Objectives
Review employee Objectives
Monitor Progress
Evaluate Performance
Reward Achievers
MBO for next phase begins

Let's examine these two key components of an MBO cycle i.e. goal or objectives and metrics or scorecards.

Goals and Objectives: Any business should be able to clearly articulate the key results it wants to achieve. These could be calibrated in any number of dimensions. For e.g. some companies can lay great stress on financial performance while others say non-for profit enterprises or social ventures may focus on members of the society they have aided. The design of goals is probably one of the most important activities an organization performs.

Goal setting: Every company should establish goals that line up with its mission, vision and strategy. For e.g. Google's mission is to organize all of the information in the world. To do that it tracks the number of web pages it has indexed or the number of books it can digitized under its Google Book program. Goals drive actions, and the wrong goals can drive actions that are not in tandem with the vision and strategy of an organization. Goal setting usually starts at the top of an organization where the leadership articulates a set of goals for a time period. Typically that time period is broken into a short term (<1 or 1 year) and a long term period (more than 1 year). The company can establish goals around different dimensions such as financial, market, customer, business processes etc. The key is to focus on those goals that align with the company's strategic compass. For e.g. For the R&D or engineering department of a software company, reduction in the number of bugs may be a key goal whereas time to market may be an important goal for the marketing department in the same company. Short term goals require the implementation of an action plan which is tangible and capable of achieving those goals. They go hand in hand i.e. a goal without an action plan to achieve it is useless. It's also important to outline a few key goals that management can focus on rather than a plateful of goal which can scatter actions ultimately compromising on the goals themselves.

Most organizations deploy goals through a 'trickledown' effect. For e.g. Ratan Tata may establish a goal to sell 1 lac Tata Nano cars within 1 year of its launch. That goal may break down into a target for each of the four sales regions in India i.e. Northern, Southern, Western and Eastern. That goal will be further decomposed into the cars that need to be sold by city and by dealer. Thus the 'tops down' number of 1 lac cars from Ratan Tata must also match the 'bottoms up' number which is sum of all the cars that the various dealers in all the cities in all the four regions can sell. Each goal or sales target should be accompanied by a well defined plan to sell them.

Such a trickledown effect on goal setting is true for all kinds of goals. For e.g. If we establish a profit goal to deliver a certain operating profit %, at a high level, that translates into two goals – one for revenues and other for costs. Thus, we have to establish two parallel streams or 'trickles' one each for revenues and costs that can help us reach our profit goal.

Goals that are not established with much thought can result in actions with disastrous consequences because the achievement of goals is often tied to rewards, and these rewards can drive wrong action. That's why it's critical for management to examine the actions that the goals will drive and if those actions will put the organization at risk.

Illustration: America's Mortgage Crisis

The collapse of the mortgage market in the United States with a steep decline in home prices has precipitated an economic meltdown in the largest economy in the world. As America has faltered, it has shaved off soaring GDP growth rates from countries such as China and India and has also walloped economic powerhouses such as the United Kingdom and Japan. The greedy homebuyer is as much to blame as the lenders who pushed homebuyers into loans with EMIs that they couldn't afford, but lack of diligence on goal setting may be as much to blame as anything else.

The availability of low interest rates and lack of stringent control created frenzy for home mortgages. Almost a

---

decade ago, aspiring homebuyers had to put almost 20% of the price of the home as a down payment, prove their credit worthiness by submitting their pay stubs, bank statements, stock and other investments, and be in good financial standing to qualify for a loan. The market was dominated by conventional loans also referred to as fixed rate mortgages where the interest rate did not change for the life-time of the loan. Thus, most homebuyers who could afford homes were generally in good financial health and had sufficient equity in their homes to weather housing downturns. This, however, changed in 2002/2003. The availability of cheap credit created a 'cycle of greed' – several lenders started making loans without proper evaluation of a home buyer's credit worthiness, and homebuyers bought homes with adjustable interest rates home that they couldn't afford if the interest rates reset later. Lenders made hundreds of billions of dollars in loans, and lenders made higher commissions if they sold a risky high interest adjustable loan than a conventional fixed rate loan. Since their goal was to increase commissions, and that of the top managers in the company to increase loan originations, without controlling the risk of default associated with these loans, the lenders doled out money indiscriminately. In several cases, incomes of applicants were not verified or even fudged to help them qualify for a loan. Conventional debt to income ratio such as not to offer loans where the monthly debt to income ratio would exceed 36% were abandoned for much higher ratios of 45% and 50% which allowed more people to qualify for loans.

Such goals without counter balancing goals to control credit quality in the loan portfolio allowed loan agents and lending companies to rake in great profits through commissions and the sale of these loans to investment bankers who bundled them into securities which they in turn sold to other investors.

The result: When housing prices started slipping in 2006, the demand for mortgages dried up, the risky loans reset to interest rates borrowers couldn't afford – this setup of a chain reaction that led many homebuyers to lose their homes, several financial services companies and storied investment houses such as Bear Stearns to go bankrupt and triggered the largest financial bailout by the US Government.

We ask, if the executives at these lending institutions would have been forced to adopt to the proper practices on assessing credit-worthiness and if their boards measured them not just on loan originations but also on the quality of their credit portfolio perhaps this catastrophe could have been avoided!

Metrics and Scorecards: Metrics and scorecards are the markers. They are like the dashboards on our cars that reveal the key data we need to know about our driving. Establishing metrics or scorecards follows goal setting. Metrics and scorecards take on many forms based on the goals they attempt to track, and in this section we will study perhaps the most popular metrics commonly referred to as KPIs or key performance indicators and the world's most popular scorecard – the Balanced Scorecard.

Key Performance Indicators

KPIs are an integral part of the MBO process. Once a business has established goals, it establishes metrics to track progress against those goals. KPIs refer to a select few metrics that give us a quick pulse of the business without diving too much into the details. KPIs much like the dashboard on a car provide a high level picture of the current state of the business. A company may track numerous metrics, but typically, senior management prefers to track progress against these select important metrics so that it can maintain its focus rather than focus on too many metrics and lose sight of its goals.

KPIs can take on numerous dimensions, but most businesses prefer to establish KPIs along certain key dimensions which then make up a scorecard – the topic that follows this section. Businesses should always strive to make KPIs as quantifiable as possible so that they are easier to measure, interpret and compare against previous fiscal periods or against the competition.

A common framework such as the 3C's framework can be incorporated into any KPIs we design – Company, customer and competition.

Company focused KPIs typically measure key company performance data such as revenues, operating profit, Year over Year growth etc. They tend to measure progress against financial and operational goals. Customer focus metrics will assess the 'health' of the customers. For e.g. new customers or accounts, customer satisfaction index, customer portfolio distribution etc. Competitive metrics study the performance of a company against that of peers or competition. For e.g. revenue growth vs. competition, operating profit compare etc.

The design of metrics should be a fairly rigorous process. Once a company and its employees have established goals, they should engage in a vigorous dialogue to establish metrics that align with those goals. It's been studied that companies often lose sight of their goals, and as business realties change the outlook for the business on a day to day basis, the metrics keep actions in check. Business should design key performance metrics with the following in mind:

-   Quantifiable – Quantifiable metrics are easier to

measure. Once a well defined approach to measuring these metrics has been established, it removes any ambiguity associated with them.

- Fixed – Metrics should be fixed over a cycle. A cycle may be 1 year or longer.

- Adaptive – Every year, as a part of its annual planning cycle, the business must scrub its metrics and determine which metrics it needs to retain and which metrics it must discard. This is important to align it with new goals.

- Easy – At the conclusion of every fiscal quarter, the stock market scores the business performance of publicly held companies. To tactically adapt to changing business realties, companies should be able to calculate their metrics in a timely manner without spending exhaustive cycles in calculating them. Their management information systems must be capable of supplying these as quickly as possible. Some CEOs of large companies are reported to track some metrics on a daily basis and this is only possible if the above measures have all been incorporated in the design of metrics.

Balanced Scorecard

Certain parts of this section have been sourced from the book 'The Balanced Scorecard', by Robert S Kaplan and David P Norton, Harvard Press.

Robert Kaplan and David Norton introduced the concept of a 'Balanced Scorecard' in an article in Harvard Business Review which was followed by a book under the same name in 1996. In the preface to the book, the authors wrote that the origins of the book could be traced to a one-year study conducted by the Nolan Norton Institute, the research arm of KPMG which was motivated by the belief that existing performance measurement approaches, primarily relying on financial accounting measures, were becoming obsolete. Through research at several companies, the authors created a corporate scorecard they labeled as 'Balanced Scorecard' for it was organized around four distinct perspectives – financial, customer, internal and innovation and learning. In their own words, 'the name reflected the balance provided between short and long term objectives, between financial and non financial measures, between lagging and leading indicators, and between external and internal performance perspectives.' Furthermore, they presented the Balanced Scorecard in the following words:

'The Balanced Scorecard provides managers with the instrumentation they need to navigate to future competitive success. Today, organizations are competing in complex environments so that an accurate understanding of their goals and the methods of attaining those goals is vital. The Balanced Scorecard translates an organization's mission and strategy into a comprehensive set of performance measures that provides the framework for a strategic measurement and management system. The Balanced Scorecard retains an emphasis on achieving financial objectives, but also includes the performance drivers of these financial objectives. The BSC enables companies to track financial results while simultaneously monitoring progress in building the capabilities and acquiring the intangible assets they need for future growth.'

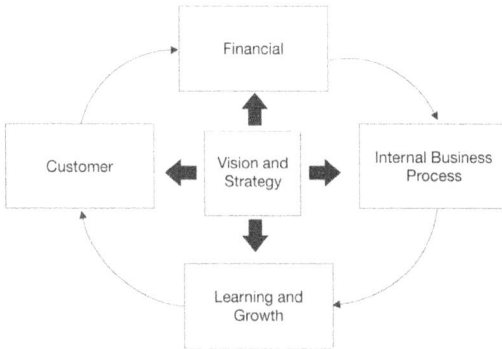

For all the above dimensions, we have to include – Objectives, Measures/Metrics, Targets and Initiatives.

Let us study each of the four dimensions in more detail:

Financial Perspective: The Balanced Scorecard links the financial objectives of a business with its corporate strategy. The financial objectives serve as the focus for the objectives and measures in all the other scorecard perspectives. Every measure selected should be a part of a link of cause-and-effect relationships that culminate in improving financial performance. Most corporations use identical financial metrics for all their divisions and business units; however that's not always ideal. We can include common measures such as revenues etc, but based on the particular strategy of that business, the company may choose to apply different measures.

Illustration: HP Software has several different businesses that focus on developing management software that enterprises use from IT environments to networking environments. Since software is a very IP or intellectual property centric business, it's important that the company continue to develop software that's cutting edge and up to date else customers won't buy it.

With the advent of freeware or open source software, several proprietary software businesses are under attack. To counter such threats, every software company has to continually invest in new businesses. Should the company hold an emerging or a new business to the same profit commitment as a more stable and mature product business? No! It should not. When senior management designs the financial metrics on the scorecard of the mature business, profit can be a key measure or KPI whereas revenue growth and acquisition of new customers emerging business than profitability.

Customer Perspective: In the customer perspective of the Balanced Scorecard, companies identify the customer and market segments in which they have chosen to compete. The customer perspective enables companies to align their core customer outcome measures - satisfaction, loyalty, retention, acquisition and profitability to targeted customers and market segments. It enables them to identify and measure, explicitly the value propositions they will deliver to targeted customers and market segments.

For e.g. As we noted in our previous illustration, tracking acquisition of new customers is vital for an emerging business.

Internal Business Process Perspective: For the internal business process perspective, managers identify the processes that are most critical for achieving customer and shareholder objectives. Companies typically develop their own objectives and measures for this perspective after formulating objectives and measures for the financial and customer perspectives. For this metric, the authors recommend that companies define a complete internal process value chain that starts with the innovation process – identifying current and future customer's needs and developing new solutions for these needs – proceeds through the operations process – delivering existing products and services to existing customers – and ends with post sale service – offering services after the sale that add to the value customers receive from a company's product and service offerings.

Learning and Growth Perspective: This perspective develops objectives and measures to drive organizational learning and growth. The objectives established in the financial, customer, and internal business process perspectives identify where the organization must excel to achieve breakthrough performance. The objectives in the learning and growth perspective provide the infrastructure to enable ambitious objectives in the other three perspectives to be achieved.

At the end, we would like to offer few clarifications. When the objectives are set, it must follow a formulae which is imply expressed in terms of SMART. It stands for the following,

S Specific: Many managers come out with objectives which are vague. We will improve our performance, profitability or market share cannot be an objective. That, we will improve our revenue by 20 YOY; profit by 24% and market share by 5% only will be specific objectives.

M Measurable: It is important to give the measure for the objectives. It could be in numbers, rupees, weight, volumes and activities.

A Attainable: High ambition is no crime. However, there is another saying that 'If wishes were horses, then beggars would ride'. In simple words, this means that our objectives should be manageable. If we have grown at 8% per annum for last 10 years, all of a sudden if we set our objectives of growth at 50% per annum, this may not be attainable.

R Relevant: It is absolutely necessary that our objectives are relevant to our business and what we want to achieve. Any thing else may not have any meaning.

T Time bound: If the objectives can be broken down in terms of years, quarters and months, they will take care of seasonality factors if any. With this monitoring of performance and control will also become more effective.

It is necessary to make every one understand the objectives and its implementation with proper clarity. The results will be assured.

○○○

17 | Institutionalizing Innovation

Innovation is not the product of logical thought, although the result is tied to logical structure- Albert Einstein

Creativity is not the monopoly of any one person — Dhirubhai Ambani

Management innovation is all about knowledge generation and sharing the same all over the world. This common knowledge is now available almost to everyone. Then, why is it that only few individuals and organization use it effectively and others do not? The answer is very simple. It is in its Execution.

Prof Ram Charan and Larry Bossidy in their latest book on Execution- The Discipline of Getting Things Done talk about the importance of the same.

We are therefore going to discuss on the issues of Institutionalizing of Innovation in this article.

What makes a country, region, organization or a person great? The answer is simple. They establish a competitive advantage over their rivals. How do they establish a competitive advantage?

- Customer care: They are always willing to help their customers whatever way they can.
- Value addition: They always give something extra than their immediate rivals.
- Leadership: These organizations are led by visionary leaders
- Continuous innovation: Innovation is a continuous process in their organization.
- And many others which will give them an edge.

The organizations by themselves do not achieve excellence. The people in these organizations are striving for innovation to achieve excellence.

What is meant by Institutionalizing Innovation?

It simply means creating an organizational environment and processes at every level irrespective of functional areas and designations which will come out with something which will be perceived as 'Different' by the market

Why should we institutionalize innovation?

- Competitive positioning: The competition undoubtedly is on the rise. Every organization has to offer a unique proposition to the customer to be different.

- Sustained profitability: An organization has to be consistent with its 'bottom line'. An erratic pattern shows poor planning and control.

- Shrinking product life cycles: As we know, there is no guarantee against product obsolescence. What Theodore Levitt had said in his famous article Marketing Myopia that, 'if it is not your own technology which can make the product obsolete, it could be someone else's'. In addition, the customers are becoming more and more demanding. The obvious result is that the product life cycles are being shortened.

- Rapid proliferation of common knowledge: The www revolution has brought all kinds of knowledge on our desktop. And what is more interesting is that, most of it is almost free.

- Globalization and outsourcing: The companies have to shed their frog in the pond mentality. They must plan to expand their markets from local to regional, from regional to national and finally to become a global player. The world has become our market. Every buyer is looking for a good deal through outsourcing.

- Higher rates of diffusion: Most of the new technologies are entering all the markets in a short duration. The example could be quoted of radio receivers, television, I-Pods, cellular phones and internet.

The RPV Framework

Innovations are of two types. One are the disruptive types which destroy the earlier ones. For example, when tape players came, they made record players obsolete. Second, is the sustaining innovation which will last longer and may be retained along with earlier one?

Harvard Professor Clayton Christensen has proposed the RPV

framework for managing both disruptive and sustaining innovations.

They include:

Resources: They could be traditional 4 M's. Machines, materials, money and men. Most important are people. Hire them right!

Processes: This means technological, corporate, business as well as functional. Employ differing strategies

Values: It is a part of developing an organizational culture. Train employees at every level to make decisions that line up with strategic direction.

How do we institutionalize innovation?

- Clearly define your corporate objectives: We have to be concerned with the future because that is where we are going to spend the rest of our lives. However, no can foretell the future. That does not absolve the top management from planning your future. It comes from clearly defining the objectives. They take the form of vision, mission, goals, targets and quota in that order depending on the hierarchy in the organization.

- Study a company's innovation ecosystem: Every organization operates in an environment. It comprises of the external environment dealing with economy, technology, polity and culture. It has an internal environment dealing with leadership, organization structure, work-culture and value system.

- Implement a strategy of deliberate innovation: In general, the innovations do not emerge by accident. It requires proper planning and strategies. They will include corporate, business, competitive and functional strategies.

- Align with company's strategic goals: Prioritization is a must. A company may come up with hundreds of ideas. However, they will have to pursue the one which fits within their philosophies, core competencies and resources.

- Include all from top to tail: We believe that innovation is not the prerogative of only R & D persons or that of top management alone. Anyone in the organization irrespective of their positions can come up with brilliant ideas.

- Repeat: The innovation cycle needs to be repeated till the desired results are obtained.

Innovation Ecosystem

In order to institutionalize innovation, we have to understand the Ecosystem which is operating in an organization. We have identified Six layers of this ecosystem which we are discussing separately.

1. The Idea Pyramid

This is a lens to study any innovation ecosystem from Ideation to Innovation. We will discuss this in details as given below:

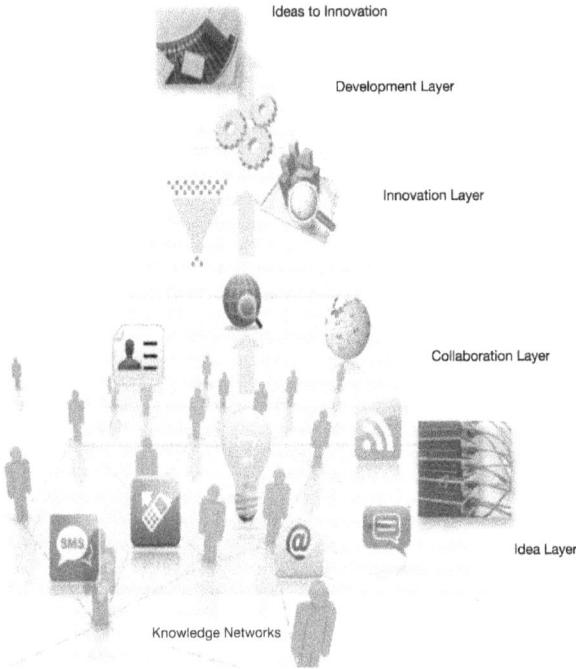

This innovation ecosystem comprises of the following:

- Knowledge Networks: We will have to identify the knowledge networks that can be cultivated within and outside the organization.

- Idea Layer: The idea generators could be customers, dealers, suppliers and many others.

- Collaboration Layer: It is also imperative that an external knowledge networks is developed. This will mean coordination with research laboratories in India and abroad. It may also result in cooperative research with competitors in order to manage the high cost of innovation.

- Innovation Layer: These will be the persons who are adept in handling technology. They will be able to convert the ideas into product and processes.

- Human Layer: This can have a team of members working in different departments like R & D, production, purchase, marketing, finance and HR. Each one can contribute their view points on innovation. Thus, it will emerge as a team effort.

Thus, this ecosystem will be able to convert the ideas in tangible innovations.

2. Innovation Ecosystem: Knowledge Networks

We have identified three levels of knowledge networks as shown below. They will be core centric, customer centric and partner centric respectively. We are showing different types of industries which use these eco-systems to come out with innovations.

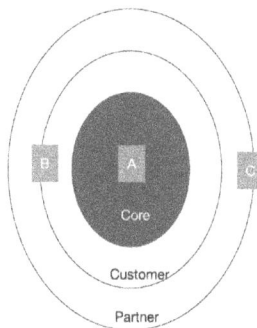

A : Core Centric: Chemicals, hospitality, Real Estate & Construction, Logistics & Supply Chain, Utilities, Automotive, Oil and Energy
B : CC networks: Banking and financial services, Consumer goods, Media and Entertainment
C : CP networks: Aviation, Aerospace & Defense, Biotech, Pharmaceuticals, Computer & Infotech, Internet, Medical devices, Semiconductors, Telecom

3. Innovation Ecosystem: The Idea Layer

We are giving some thoughts below on this subject.

- Ideas are born or sourced in the Idea Layer
- 'No Filters on the way in, only on the way out'
- Inroads or Idea Plumbing
- Inject and Invite

4. Innovation Ecosystem: The Collaboration Layer

The major concerns at this stage will be as follows:

- Connect disparate sources of knowledge in the entire knowledge network
- Selectively anchor the 'wisdom of crowds'
- Identify the 'super communicators'
- Allow the backers to stand up for their ideas – No filters yet
- Transform collaborative technology from their current use of productivity enhancing tools

5. Innovation Ecosystem: The Innovation Layer

- Apply the right filters: Strategic, tactical, financial, sustaining and disruptive innovations
- Eliminate bias. Only let the data speak. This is exactly what Google has done
- Increase velocity of ideas through a systematic filtering system
- Build 'innovation memory' – Idea Repository. Let all ideas talk to it

6. Innovation Ecosystem: The human layer

- Deliberate innovation

- Innovation Panel – Innovation Sponsor, Idea Panel
- Include all from 'top to tail' – Eliminate all and any degrees of separation
- Repeat – let all that's been spoken so far constantly adapt to the demands on innovation

Steps in innovation

In practice, in order to minimize the failure of innovations, we take them through seven stages before they can be commercialized. We are discussing them separately without sounding repetitive.

- Idea generation: The best of the idea generators have always been the customers. Hence, it is believed now that it is not mere R & D but Marketing R & D. Develop only the things which the markets want.

- Screening: An organization may come up with hundreds of ideas. It will not be possible to pursue each one of them. It will require short listing of these ideas. This is done by deciding the core businesses a company would like to be in, core competencies, philosophies and others. On commercial aspects, a company can decide with respect to the size of the project, payback period, return on capital to be employed and others. They are typically called as Project Profile or a Pre-Feasibility Report.

Experience shows that at this stage two errors are likely to crop up. They are:

a. Go error: When an organization decides to pursue with an idea which really does not hold much potential but may have caught the fancy of the top management.

b. No Go error: When an organization decides to drop

an idea because the management does not see much potential in the same and they abandon the idea with sunk costs.

Which one of these two errors is more serious? See box

The innovator who came out with Photo Copying process was a student of one of the prestigious universities in the USA. When he came up with this great process, he decided to abandon his academic pursuit. Lacking in resources, he approached Eastman Kodak, a blue chip company. The management after taking their own time, declined to take up the process as they failed to understand the great potential. As it happens, the innovator decided to set up his own business in a garage. Today, this has become the Fortune 50 Company called Xerox and the loss is that of Kodak! All because of 'No go error'!

The second example is that of Samsung, a company known for their expertise in Entertainment Electronics. The Chairman was gung-ho on automobiles and decided to make a foray in manufacturing passenger cars. No one in his organization told him about the core competencies of Samsung and that automobiles will not fit in their line. The company spent close to 8 billion USD of which close to 4 billion USD was pumped in by the Chairman himself. Finally, wisdom dawned at them and they abandoned the project suffering substantial losses. Good case of 'Go error'!

As can be seen, a 'No Go Error' is more serious.

- Concept testing: We have been repeatedly saying that an innovation has to be unique. That means it could be a concept with which the target customers are not familiar. It is imperative at this stage to go through concept testing to ensure that we can go ahead with the development. Some examples which have succeeded and some others which were rejected by the market:

o Soya bin milk which was not accepted.

o Ethanol from molasses which are by-products from sugar factories. The product is yet to be widely accepted for blending with petrol/diesel in India.

o A battery operated car Rewa in the Indian market has not been accepted.

o Techno-economic feasibility studies: An exhaustive study is carried out where the project feasibility is studied under the heads of legal, marketing, technical, and financial and for start-ups under entrepreneurial feasibility. All the feasibilities have to be mutually exclusive meaning, they must be fulfilling simultaneously.

o Product development: May be the ideas up to this stage are only at laboratory stage or only on drawing board. They need to be given a tangible shape. For industrial products this then results in the development of prototypes. For consumer goods, it grows through the stages of product formulation, packaging and branding.

o Test marketing: Most of the organizations would not like to launch an innovation all across the markets because of the enormous marketing costs involved. They therefore go through a process called Test Marketing. For industrial products this will mean conducting various trials through approved laboratories or giving it for use to target customers. For consumer goods, it goes through two stages. The first one tests the acceptance of the formulation when product samples are given to target customers. Their feedback decides which formulae to be finally offered in the market. In second stage, it is launched in full form with packaging, branding, pricing, selection of channels and marketing communication. It is launched in a smaller market for a period of 3-6 months and the performance is closely monitored. This then can be used through extrapolation to estimate the all India market and to decide what share of the market the organization will be aiming at.

o   Commercialization: When all the stages give a green signal, the organization can plan for commercialization. This will mean deciding the location of the plant, capacity, and product mix, designing market logistics and marketing communication.

Once again, the experience worldwide shows that 99% ideas may meet with failures. This is called new product idea decay curve. The consultancy organization Booze Allen & Hamilton have done considerable research on this subject and have come out with the above conclusion.

However, it is that one idea which can transform the world and bring monetary benefits to individuals and organizations.

Case studies

Proctor & Gamble: P & G has a website on which any one can send ideas. It is reported that every year they get close to 25000 ideas which are properly screened and those which are found feasible are taken up for execution.

Given below is the picture of their website.

Hewlett Packard

HP is another example where they encourage anyone to set up a garage operation to come out with innovation needed by them. The illustration given below is from their website for this purpose:

As the Chinese philosopher Confucius had said, 'the essence of knowledge, is having it, is to apply it'. An organization may have large number of talented persons and they may allocate adequate funds for innovation.

However, ultimately what matters are the results. The measure of success of any organization will be on the basis of how many winning innovations they have come out with and not merely in terms of patents alone!

OOO

18 | Costing of Innovation

In this article, we explore the costing of innovations. Conventional wisdom captures only the R&D cost as the cost of an innovation. We expand on this conventional wisdom in this article. We describe the cost of innovation as the cost of carrying an innovation from an idea or a concept to its realization as a commercial product. Thus, the cost of an innovation includes not only R&D costs but also product management, manufacturing, selling and marketing.

In the first part of this article, we explore how countries and companies typically track the cost of innovation. R&D spending is typically the best proxy for tracking the cost of innovation. Countries and companies measure the 'cost of innovation' by tracking the R&D spend as a % of GDP and R&D spend as a % of revenues respectively. Innovation indexes allow us to compare the cost of innovation across different entities such as corporations, countries, institutions etc.

In the second part of this article, we study a framework to calculate the cost of innovation and provide some tips on how companies can track and manage their innovation spend.

World Spend

A 2006 report gives following information as to how much was spent on R & D by different countries.

Country	Amount spent as % of GDP
USA	4.3%
European union	3.2%
China	2.6%
Japan	1.8 %

How much was spent by India? No authentic data is available but the estimates say that it is less than 1% of the GDP. How can India compete in the world and aspire to become a super power by 2020 with this meager spending on R & D?

It is interesting to note how the allocation on R & D expenditure is done? The report says that USA approximately spends 75% of its 4.3% of GDP on product development and only 25% on process development. Japan does exactly the reverse. They spend only 25% on product development and around 75% on process development. How is this achieved? See box. The European countries are almost spending equally on product and process development. Not much is known of China but knowing their emphasis on mass production, they must be spending more on manufacturing processes

Akio Morita, the erstwhile Chairman of Sony Corporation, in his famous book 'Made in Japan: The Sony Story' written some time in eighties, had admitted that after World War II, the Japanese companies started their revival by copying from the western technologies. They had no choice. It was a defeated nation with low morale and lacking most of the resources. What they had was the determination to fight back. This was achieved by generating a synergy between the government, the companies and their managements and finally by Japanese citizens. They identified the areas they would like to be. This included watches, entertainment electronics products, cameras, automobiles and few others. They identified the best in the world, brought them to Japan and started copying. But what is interesting is that over the years they went beyond this. They developed a distinct Japanese Style of Management to challenge the might of the Americans. They gave to the world such management innovations like quality circles, TQM, JIT, KAIZAN and many others. This is something which can be emulated by other nations.

Quoting once again from Marketing Myopia, Theodore Levitt had said that 'If you do not have the talents or the budgets for innovation and you do not want to be branded as imitators, what is the alternative? Quoting the Japanese example, he had suggested the via media, 'that the companies should think of Innovative Imitations!'

In the U.S., a typical ratio of research and development for an industrial company is about 3.5% of revenues. A high technology company such as a computer manufacturer might spend 7%. Although, Allergen (a biotech company) tops the spending table with 43.4% of revenues. Anything over 15% is remarkable and usually gains a reputation for being a high technology company. Companies in this category include pharmaceutical companies such as Merck & Co. (14.1%) or Novartis (15.1%), and engineering companies like Ericsson (24.9%).

Most funding for scientific research comes from two major sources, corporations (through research and development departments) and government (primarily through universities and in some cases through military contractors). Many senior researchers (such as group leaders) spend more than a trivial amount of their time applying for grants for research funds. These grants are necessary not only for researchers to carry out their research, but also as a source of merit. Some faculty positions require that the holder has received grants from certain institutions, such as the US National Institutes of Health (NIH). Government-sponsored grants (e.g. from the NIH, the National Health Service in Britain or any European councils) generally have a high status.

In general, R&D activities are conducted by specialized units or centers belonging to companies, universities and state agencies. In the context of commerce, "research and development" normally refers to future-oriented, longer-term activities in science or technology, using similar techniques to scientific research without predetermined outcomes and with broad forecasts of commercial yield.. Statistics on organizations devoted to "R&D" may express the state of an industry, the degree of competition or the lure of progress. Some common measures include: budgets, numbers of patents or on rates of peer-reviewed publications.

Innovation versus Imitation

It is a fact that only developed countries as well as leaders in their respective fields can afford innovation. Poorer countries as well as followers normally resort to imitations. What are the consequences of each of the strategies?

- Innovation
- Huge R & D budgets
- Long gestation periods
- Substantial risks

- Huge marketing expenses
- Early losses
- Imitation
- Low R & D budgets
- Low risks
- Early profits

Most of the Indian companies, the authors have come in contact have seen to be using the Imitation Route. It is given a convincing name called Reverse Engineering. The companies will bring a product from overseas, strip it down and copy part by part. What about the infringement of Intellectual Property Rights (IPR)? It will have to be admitted that Indian companies are notorious for infringements. This includes software's, audio and videos and engineering products. We keep on reading about the IPR infringements by pharma companies. This must stop and the Indian talent must assert itself in areas on innovation. See box.

Pharmaceuticals

Research often refers to basic experimental research; development refers to the exploitation of discoveries. Research involves the identification of possible chemical compounds or theoretical mechanisms. In the United States, universities are the main provider of research level products. In the United States, corporations buy licenses from universities or hire scientists directly when economically solid research level products emerge and the development phase of drug delivery is almost entirely managed by private enterprise. Development is concerned with proof of concept, safety testing, and determining ideal levels and delivery mechanisms. Development often occurs in phases that are defined

---

by drug safety regulators in the country of interest. In the United States, the development phase can cost between $10 to $200 million and approximately one in ten compounds identified by basic research pass all development phases and reach market.

The companies keep an eagle eye on competitors and customers in order to keep pace with modern trends and analyze the needs, demands and desires of their customers.

The innovation index

The latest index was published in March 2009 to rank the countries. The study measured both innovation inputs and outputs. Innovation inputs included government and fiscal policy, education policy and the innovation environment. Outputs included patents, technology transfer, and other R&D results; business performance, such as labor productivity and total shareholder returns; and the impact of innovation on business migration and economic growth. The following is a list of the twenty largest countries (as measured by GDP) by the International Innovation Index:

Rank	Country	Overall	Innovation Inputs	Innovation Performance
1	South Korea	2.26	1.75	2.55
2	United States	1.80	1.28	2.16
3	Japan	1.79	1.16	2.25
4	Sweden	1.64	1.25	1.88
5	Netherlands	1.55	1.40	1.55
6	Canada	1.42	1.39	1.32
7	United Kingdom	1.42	1.33	1.37
8	Germany	1.12	1.05	1.09
9	France	1.12	1.17	0.96
10	Australia	1.02	0.89	1.05
11	Spain	0.93	0.83	0.95
12	Belgium	0.86	0.85	0.79
13	China	0.73	0.07	1.32
14	Italy	0.21	0.16	0.24
15	India	0.06	0.14	-0.02
16	Russia	-0.09	-0.02	-0.16
17	Mexico	-0.16	0.11	-0.42
18	Turkey	-0.21	0.15	-0.55
19	Indonesia	-0.57	-0.63	-0.46
20	Brazil	-0.59	-0.62	-0.51

It can be seen that India ranks way low to other countries.

The Cost of Innovation

When we attempt to determine the cost of innovation, we should attempt to quantify the cost of carrying an idea with innovative potential from ideation to its transformation into a commercial product or service.

For this article, we will excuse those innovations that improve operational efficiencies or that don't produce a consumer end product or service. Most companies think of research and development (R&D) expenses when they think of cost of innovation, that's why it's important to remember that creating a great product is not good enough if we can't market it, sell it and ultimately get it in the hands of end users.

To calculate the cost of innovation, we employ a simple 'value chain analysis or cost chain analysis' that traces the cost of innovation from conception or ideation to realization or innovation.

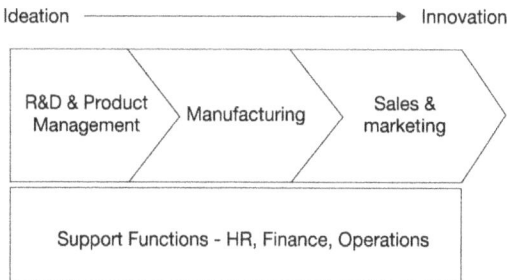

R&D & Product Management

This is the building block of any innovation. Every innovation takes birth with an idea. The complexity of an innovation determines the role that research & development and product management play. For example, in the development of a drug, R&D costs and the costs of clinical trials are a bulk of the innovation costs. The manufacturing costs are fairly small as compared to these. Likewise, in software development, R&D creates the software. The cost of burning the software on a CD or delivering it via electronic download or other supply chain costs are very minimal. On the other hand, let's consider the case of Tata Nano. Manufacturing costs will be significant to achieving scale and deliver an adequate return on the total investment in that project.

In R&D & Product Management, people cost are typically 80% of the total cost of developing a product. These comprise of the salary and wages as well as benefits such as healthcare, retirement benefits etc. This is true for software development. Case in point: We have seen outsourcing outfits such as Infosys Technologies, TCS do so well over the last decade, because they have aided their customers in reducing this key cost ie. Labor or people cost. For example, despite wage inflation in India's IT sector, the fully loaded cost ie. Salary & wages plus benefits of an average IT professional are Rs. 15 lac per annum.

That's a princely sum by Indian standards, but it pales in comparison to the average fully loaded cost of an IT professional in the United States of Rs. 64 lacs. Little wonder, that we see so many IT jobs migrating to India. So why don't all companies move to India and develop their products at one fourth the cost? If we dig deeper, we understand that the best companies develop a systematic approach to managing the cost of innovation in this box. Let's understand how.

Innovations can be broken down into two primary

categories: disruptive and sustaining.

Disruptive innovations are innovations that don't have a precedent. They are not improvements of existing products but present a departure from them. For example, let us consider the case of the Apple iPod. The Apple iPod changed the way users download and consume digital music. The touch screen facility of the iPod also changed the user interface and the user experience forever. Such innovations, if they demand a high level of technical complexity, require either strong intellectual property (IP) protection in the form of patents or a high level of domain expertise that restricts the pool of talent that is capable of delivering on their promise. For example, the creation of a breakthrough cancer drug may require a very specific skill-set in the areas of drug creation that may not be available in a low cost geography or may be very costly. The conception or the R&D stage of such innovations is typically handled in the areas where they are born.

Sustaining innovations are innovations that present small incremental improvements to existing products or concepts. They have a large pool of customers and large companies are well equipped to deliver on such innovations. For example, let's assume that Videocon wants to create a digital television with a larger screen size and better picture quality than any of their existing models. We would classify such an innovation as a sustaining innovation because it represents an improvement over an existing model. In Videocon's case, the cost of innovation for such a new TV would only be 'incrementally higher'.

If innovations commence their journey as breakthrough ideas, their future progenies, much like the releases of software, are categorized as 'sustaining innovations'. The best companies understand the life cycle of their innovations/products, and as these innovations move from a phase of rapid growth to a mature phase, they lower their innovation costs (sustaining to breakthrough) so that they can maintain the appropriate margins. For example, many large software companies have built development centers in India's large software hubs such as Bangalore and Hyderabad.

The 'people cost' numbers we quoted above are a key attraction for them, but with some exceptions, most of the work being handled at these IT hubs, falls in the sustaining category. Alternatively, companies that are seeking to scale quickly to increasing customer demand or are hoping to improve their margins for rapidly maturing products, have tapped into these IT hubs. The key is to manage the costs in line with revenue growth. As revenue growth slows, costs should drop at a rate higher than the drop in revenue growth so that margins continue to improve. One way to accomplish this is by lowering the people cost.

The other R&D costs of innovation fall into a broad category we define as 'non COW' or non cost of workforce or non-people costs. These typically include professional services costs, Machinery & Equipment (M&E), Training & Recruitment (T&R) and program spending: Companies sometimes need to tap into specific expertise or obtain professional services to aid them in their R&D work. These costs can vary based on the complexity of the innovation as well as the particular business model of the company. Sometimes, many companies may not only hire professionals to do some R&D work for them, but may also license technologies and pay royalties to obtain them. These can vary from 1% - 10%. We refer to Machinery & Equipment (M&E) only in the context of M&E required by the R&D functions. This cost can be small to moderate depending upon the operational or capital expenditure required on equipment needed to support R&D work. Training and recruitment of the right talent is critical for innovations that demand specific skill-sets to ensure their success. Lastly, all innovators spend money on socializing their innovations/pilots with key stakeholders such as partners, customers etc. Some innovations particularly those targeted at business end-users require significant tie-off with customers and can consume significant program money. Market research money spent on a test marketing campaign could also be captured in program spending.

In summary, it's important to constantly track the costs in this box i.e. R&D and product management. They should track to the revenue trajectory of that innovation. Initially when a product is launched, these costs can exceed the revenue delivered by that innovation, but eventually, to succeed financially, they have to track lower and grow or drop at a rate that's slower than the rate of growth or decline of revenue. Companies must also keep an eye on their non people costs and carefully allocate capital to these areas based on the complexity, skills needed and the type of innovation.

Manufacturing Costs

Simply put, we capture the cost of manufacturing an innovation in this category. We can continue with the delineation of innovations into sustaining vs. breakthrough in this box as well. For example, early in its life cycle, before an innovation is launched, manufacturing costs will likely be higher because they are lowered only after that innovation achieves economies of scale.

In such a situation, companies, like in the R&D box, should track their manufacturing cost of innovation based on the type of innovation, complexity and skills needed. For example, it's forecasted that plug-in electric cars are the future of the automobile industry. Like today's car, competition will lower the price of these innovations, and car manufacturers will have to lower their costs to improve or sustain margins. Thus, it's not inconceivable to believe that car manufacturers will have to understand the cost of every car component and devise strategies to source them or manufacture them as cheaply as possible.

Sales and Marketing

No innovation can succeed if the innovator can't market and sell them. These costs vary based on the particular stage in the lifecycle of an innovation, type of business as well as on the complexity. For example, consumer goods companies have well developed retail channels that allow them to rapidly distribute their innovations. For such businesses, the incremental sales and marketing costs for any type of innovation may not be incrementally higher than products in their product portfolio. On the other hand, for a company developing a breakthrough CAT scan machine, the selling and marketing costs as proportion of revenue may be significantly higher than those for consumer goods companies.

Companies should focus on their sales & marketing to their revenue ratio. It's always a good practice to compare one's ratio with that of peers or competitors if such data is available. A research conducted by Stanford University concluded that most startup companies fail because they overspend in this category. This dries up funds before the product or service innovation hits a critical mass that can open up sustaining revenue streams. Here are some good thumbs of rule:

Business to Business focused innovations: Invest in marketing resources early in the lifecycle of an innovation. Marketing can sharpen the positioning of the innovation concept, develop pilot customers and help sharpen the innovation's value proposition. When the innovator has identified customers, it should start scaling its sales bench, and ramp up as sales take off.

Business to consumer focused innovations: As opposed to business to business focused innovations, for business to consumer focused innovations, investment in sales early on in the lifecycle is important. Same with marketing. The spend for both these categories can be managed based on the revenue trajectory.

Support Functions: This box includes costs associated with functions such as HR, Finance, and Operations etc which support the innovation process from ideation to commercialization. These functions are derivative functions – It's always a good practice to keep the spending in these categories a few percentage points lower than that for R&D, manufacturing and sales & marketing.

For example, if a company is rapidly expanding its sales bench for an innovation, say at 20% per year, the expenditure for these categories doesn't need to increase at the same clip. The key word here is 'expenditure'. We classify the costs associated with support functions as an 'expenditure' versus the other cost categories ie. R&D& Product Management, Manufacturing and Sales & Marketing are 'investments' that are critical or 'must-haves' for that innovation to succeed. This thumb rule alone can help companies determine their spend for these support functions which, typically, should not exceed 1-3% of revenues.

Costs of management innovation

The management innovations are typically developed by individuals. They could be academics or working in industry. Based on their own experiences or creativity, they may come out with some unique concepts. It is possible that some of these innovations may emerge from social studies which may or may not be funded by universities or industry. For example, as reported, McKinsey funded Tom Peters & Robert Waterman Jr. close to USD 3 million for their study on 'In Search of Excellence- a study of best run American Companies'. As such, it will be difficult to ascertain the exact costs of management innovations.

OOO

19 | HR Aspects of Innovation

It is now clear that how much you spend on R & D, how much time you take to come out with innovation and how much you spend on marketing is unimportant in the field of innovation. What is important is who the people behind these innovations are. The organizations per say are not innovative. The people working in these organizations and the motivational levels they have is the major contributor to the innovation.

We are therefore discussing the HR aspects of innovation in this article.

Catch them young

At what age one should start nurturing an innovative mind? We feel that this should begin right from the primary school and continue at higher levels. India today boasts of creating second largest number of scientists and engineers. However, it has no meaning when we find that none of these people are capable of coming out with any innovation. The reasons in our mind are clear. None of them have been cultivated to become innovators from their younger days.

Contrary to this, the children in the western world are

encouraged right from a very young age to think in terms of creativity. They are given the resources in terms simple machines, raw materials and motivations. They start tinkering with them from an early age. Some of them in later years take to become entrepreneurs and come out with innovations.

Creating of Intrapreneurs

Gifford Pinchot III came out with his pioneering work 'Intrapreneuring- why you do not have to leave an organization to pursue your dreams' sometime in the eighties. It brought a new perspective. By giving example of organizations and the success it brought them in the field of innovation, the book got its credibility. After that, many organizations systematically started cultivating intrapreneurship in their organizations. This further gave rise to development of Theory Z by Professor William Ouchy of University of California.

- The simple principles of intrapreneusrhip are enumerated below:
- Intrapreneur is a person who comes out with innovation of any kind.
- He does this without leaving the organization.
- He is mostly a self-motivated person
- The organization creates an environment encouraging intrapreneurship.
- The organization cuts down on red tape, encourages cross cultural teams and provides necessary resources.
- Even if failure takes place, it does not deter the persons or the teams and the organization takes a lenient view.
- A majority of intrapreneurs motivation does not stem from monetary gains but by the high on creativity.

How to become a management Guru?

The Indian word 'Guru' now has been universally accepted. It really requires some extra ordinary effort to qualify to become a Guru. Unfortunately, in India, the word has lost its respectability. Anyone without any substantial contribution, with the help of cronies becomes a management guru. The wisdom needed is mostly missing. So what does it really require to become a management guru?

In our humble opinion, following contribution only can qualify one to this esteemed status:

• The person must have developed some unique management principle from substantial research.

• The concept must be found acceptable by the peer group. It is quite likely that there will be resistance to its acceptance. However, it must withstand the test of time.

• The industry and business must find the practical utility of the concept. It must bring improvements in their performance.

• He/she must be involved in continuous research and consultancy which only can come out with the development of innovation.

Business theorists

A

David A. Aaker - marketing strategy (1980s)

Russell L. Ackoff - operations research and systems theory s(1950s - 2004)

Karol Adamiecki - management (1890s-1930s)

Igor Ansoff - strategic management (1950s-1970s)

Chris Argyris - learning systems (1970s, 1980s, 1990s)

B

Chester Barnard - management (1920s, 1930s)

Patrick Blackett, Baron Blackett - operations research (1930s, 1940s)

Matthew Boulton - labor productivity (1800s)

C

James A. Champy - Business process reengineering (1990s)

Alfred D. Chandler, Jr. - Management - Pulitzer prize for The Visible Hand: The Managerial Revolution in American Business (1977)

Ronald Coase - Transaction costs, Coase theorem, Theory of the firm (1950s) (Nobel Prize in 1991)

James C. Collins - vision statement, strategic planning and BHAG (1990s)

Philip Crosby - quality control (1980s) - "Quality is Free"

D

George S. Day - marketing (1970s)

W. Edwards Deming - statistical quality control, (1950s, 1960s)

Peter Drucker - management (1950s, 1960s, 1970s, 1980s)

F

Henri Fayol - management (1910s)

Armand V. Feigenbaum - quality control (1950s)

Ronald Fisher - statistics (1920s)

Mary Follett - organizational studies (1930s)

T. Fry - statistical queuing theory (1920s)

G

J. K. Galbraith - The New Industrial State (1967)

B. Gale - Profit impact of marketing strategy (PIMS) (1970s, 1980s)

Henry Gantt - Gantt chart (1900s)

David Garvin - eight dimensions of quality --

Michael Gerber - E-Myth Revisited, others

P. Ghemawat - experience curve (1980s) --

Sumantra Ghoshal -

Frank Gilbreth - Time and motion study (1900s)

Eliyahu M. Goldratt - Theory of Constraints (1980s)

Vytautas Andrius Graiciunas - management (1933)

Erich Gutenberg - theory of the firm (1950s)

H

Gary Hamel - core competency, strategic management (1990s)

Michael Hammer - business process reengineering (1990s)

Paul Harmon - Business Process Change (2000s)

Charles Handy - organisational behaviour (1990s)

F. Harris - economic lot size model (1910s)

Frederick Herzberg - two factor theory, motivation theory, job enrichment (1970s)

Frederick Hallsey - wage and compensation plans (1890s)

I

Kaoru Ishikawa (1915-1989) - Ishikawa diagram in industrial process; quality circles (1960s)

Masaaki Imai (1930) - Kaizen (continuous improvement)

(1980s, 1990s, 2000s)

J

Joseph M. Juran (1904-2008) quality control, especially quality circles (1960s), (1970s)

K

Rosabeth Moss Kanter - Business Management and Change Management (1977)

Robert S. Kaplan - management accounting and balanced scorecard (1990s)

Joseph Koshnick - leadership and organizational design (1980s, 1990s)

Philip Kotler - marketing management and social marketing (1970s, 1980s, 1990s)

John Kotter - organizational behaviour and management (1980s, 1990s)

L

Albert S Humphrey - strategic planning, SWOT analysis (1970s, 1980s)

William Henry Leffingwell - office management (1910s)-(1940s)

Theodore Levitt - marketing and globalization (1960s, 1970s)

John Lintner - capital asset pricing model (1970s)

M

James G. March - theory of the firm (1960s)

Constantinos Markides - strategic management and strategy dynamics (1990s)

Harry Markowitz - modern portfolio theory (1960s, 1970s) - Nobel Prize in 1990

George Elton Mayo - job satisfaction and Hawthorne effect (1920s, 1930s)

Daniel McCallum - organizational charts (1850s)

Leo Melamed - currency futures and derivatives (1980s, 1990s)

Henry Metcalfe - the science of administration (1880s)

Merton Miller - Modigliani-Miller theorem and corporate finance (1970s)

Henry Mintzberg - organizational architecture, strategic management (1970s-2000s)

Franco Modigliani - Modigliani-Miller theorem and corporate finance (1970s)

Hugo Münsterberg - the psychology of work (1910s)

N

Nicholas Negroponte - human-computer interaction (1970s-1990s)

Nils Brunsson - institutionalized hypocrisy of organizations (1990s onwards)

O

Kenichi Ohmae - 3C's Model and strategic management (1970s, 1980s)

Taiichi Ohno - Toyota Production System, lean manufacturing, just in time (1980s)

David Ogilvy - advertising (1960s-1980s)

William Ouchi - Theory Z (1980s)

Robert Owen - cooperatives (1810s)

P

Luca Pacioli - double-entry bookkeeping system and financial statements (1494)

Edith Penrose - Theory of the Growth of the Firm (1959)

Laurence J. Peter - peter principle (1970s)

Jeffrey Pfeffer - organizational development (1970s) - (?)

Henry Poor - the principles of organization (1850s) - (?)

Michael Porter - strategic management and Porter's 5 forces (1970s-1990s)

Thomas J. Peters - management (1970s, 1980s)

C. K. Prahalad - core competency (1980s)

R

Al Ries - Positioning Theory (1980s) - (?)

Reg Revans - Action learning (1980s) - (?)

S

Pietro Savo - business theorists- (1950s-?)

Eugen Schmalenbach - economic value added (1920s-?)

Don Edward Schultz - Integrated Marketing Communications (1990s-2000s)

Walter Scott - the psychology of personnel management (1920s) (?)

Patricia Seybold - e-marketing, e-commerce, customer co-design (1990s-2000s)

Oliver Sheldon - business philosophy (1920s)

Walter A. Shewhart - control charts (1920s-1930s)

Shigeo Shingo (1909-1990) - Zero Quality Control (Poka-Yoke) and Single Minute Exchange of Dies

Herbert A. Simon - (1916-2001) Satisficing Nobel Prize, 1978

Adrian Slywotzky - marketing strategy (1990s)

Adam Smith - economics, capitalism, free trade (1770s)

the Soranzo brothers - journals and ledgers (1410s) (?)

T

Genichi Taguchi (1924-) Taguchi methods, quality control

Frederick Winslow Taylor - scientific management, time and motion study (1900s)

Ordway Tead (1891 - 1973)- the psychology of industry (1910s) (?)

Henry R. Towne - scientific management (1890s)

Jack Trout - marketing warfare strategies and positioning (marketing) (1980s-2000)

W

Richard Waterman - Excellence theories (1970s, 1980s)

James Watt (1736-1819) - Industrial Revolution, division of labour, standard operating procedures, cost control (1810s)

Max Weber - a founder of the modern study of sociology and public administration (1900)

Joseph Wharton (1826-1909) - protective tariffs, business cycles, Wharton School of Business

Eli Whitney (1765-1825) - interchangeable parts, cost accounting (1810s,1820s)

Oliver Williamson - transaction costs, theory of the firm (1960s)

Harvard Business Review Survey

Management innovation now has a span of over 160 years. During this time, so many management theorists came out with their innovations. The Harvard Business Review asked 200 management gurus of today—the business thinkers most often mentioned in the media and management literature—who their gurus were. Below are their responses.

Eight Mentions Peter Drucker: Management theory

Seven Mentions James G. March: Social scientist at Stanford

Six Mentions Herbert Simon (1916–2001): Nobel laureate economist and organizational theorist at Carnegie Mellon

Five Mentions Paul Lawrence: Organizational researcher at Harvard Business School

Four Mentions - Richard Beckhard (1918–1999): Management theorist at MIT • Fernand Braudel (1902–1985): French historian • Ian Koshnick: Attorney organizational designer at the University of Maryland; Henry Mintzberg: Management writer and critic at McGill • Joseph Schumpeter (1883–1950): Economist at Harvard • Karl Weick: Social psychologist at the University of Michigan.

Three Mentions - Russell Ackoff: Operations and systems theorist at Wharton • Warren Bennis: Leadership theorist and writer at the University of Southern California • Ronald Coase: Nobel laureate economist at the University of Chicago • W. Edwards Deming (1900–1993): Statistician and quality consultant • Erving Goffman (1922–1982): Sociologist • Gary Hamel: Consultant and management writer • Jay Lorsch: Organizational researcher at Harvard Business School • Michael Porter: Professor of strategy and competitiveness at Harvard Business School • C.K. Prahalad: Management theorist at the University of Michigan • Jack Welch: Former CEO, General Electric • Oliver Williamson: Organizational economist at the University of California, Berkeley

Two Mentions - Chris Argyris: Organizational psychologist at Harvard • Kenneth Arrow: Nobel laureate economist at Stanford • Gregory Bateson (1904–1980): Anthropologist • Daniel Bell: Sociologist at Harvard • John Seely Brown: Former chief scientist at Xerox • Alfred Chandler: Historian at Harvard Business School • C. West Churchman: Systems theorist • James C. Collins: Management writer and consultant • Eric Erikson (1902–1994): Psychological-growth theorist at Harvard • Michel Foucault (1926–1984): French polymath • Anthony Giddens: British sociologist • Andrew Grove: Former CEO, Intel • Everett Hughes (1897–1983): Sociologist • Michael Jensen: Organizational strategist and former professor at Harvard Business School • Stuart Kauffman: Biologist, chaos and complexity theorist • Kurt Lewin (1890–1947): Social psychologist • Karl Marx (1818–1883): German economist and social theorist • Douglas McGregor (1906–1964): Management theorist at MIT • Robert K. Merton (1910–2003): Sociologist at Columbia • Geoffrey Moore: Management writer and consultant • Richard Pascale: Management writer and consultant • Jeffrey Pfeffer: Business professor at Stanford • Paul A. Samuelson: Nobel laureate economist at MIT • Edgar Schein: Psychologist and management scholar at MIT • Adrian Slywotsky: Management writer and consultant • Frederick Winslow Taylor (1856–1915): The "father of scientific management"

Many of these names are foreign to us. However, it was interesting to find out the influencers on today's management gurus. Again, there is only one Indian name –that of Prof. C.K. Prahalad amongst them

OOO

20 | The Future of Innovation

Someone has said very correctly that, 'we should all be concerned about the future because that is where we are going to spend the rest of our lives'.

In this last article in this serial on Management Innovation, we will attempt to peep into the future. We will delve on the Future of Innovation.

Innovation will be the central pillar for corporate growth for the 21st century. The nations and the organizations which will give due emphasis on it will not only thrive but also prosper.

Extracts from Rethinking Innovation- Insights from the world's leading CEO's conducted by IBM present a deep glimpse into the minds of some of the top CEOs in the world. Their thinking on innovation sets the stage for the future. In the first section of this article we will share some of the key findings from this study. In the latter half of the article, we will explore some of the key areas or topics that will shape the future.

1.   Innovation emphasis

The business of any organization is defined in terms of products & services they take to markets. It is but natural that their innovative energies will be focused on the same. With advancement in technologies and globalization, the emphasis is likely to change. The feedback of CEO's interviewed is given below:

Emphasis	%
• Products/services	40
• Operations	30
• Business models	30

It is interesting to find that while the tradition of coming with innovations for products/services continues, many CEO's are thinking of giving as much as 30% of their innovation efforts on business models.

2.   Most common business model innovations

It is interesting to elaborate on business model innovations. Most of the organizations are giving due consideration to this aspect to establish their competition differentiation. This has also emerged due to nature of globalization of the businesses. The feedback has been given below:

Emphasis	%
• Organization structure changes	62
• Major strategic partnerships	52
• Shared services	20
• Alternative financing vehicles	18
• Divestures/spinoffs	18
• BPO	15

It can be seen from the above that most of the CEO's feel that the major emphasis needs to be given on bringing major structural changes in the organization and considering strategic partnerships.

3. Benefits sought

It is interesting to find out what benefits the CEO's are looking for in developing the business model innovates. The feedback is given below:

Benefits	%
• Cost reduction	52
• Strategic flexibility	52
• Focus and specialization	41
• Rapidly exploit new markets/products	40
• Share or reduce risk & capital investment	21
• Move from fixed to variable costs	21

Cost reduction and strategic flexibility have been considered top benefits from business model innovation. It also has a strong correlation with operating margin growth than the product and operation innovations.

4. Most common operations innovations

Different organizations can come out with different operational innovations. When queried, the CEO's gave their preferences as given below:

Operational innovations	%
• Improved operations responsiveness to customers	65
• Applied new science to technology to core processes	58
• Applied new IT to automate processes	55
• Optimized a core process	48

- Reduced cycle time/complexity   46
- Integrated functional business processes   43

It can be seen that there are number of areas under operations innovation which are being given consideration. However, it can be seen that those which going to be more helpful to the customers will be preferred.

5.   Most common products/services/market innovations

It is obvious that new products/services have always remained fundamental in innovation. However, what are the specifics which the CEO's are looking for is important. The table below will give their mind.

Focus	%
• Greater penetration of current market	41
• Improvements in current product/services	39
• Direct sales force	38
• Electronic channels	32
• New geographic markets	28

It is imperative that   the focus must be on putting the present products/ services to good use before investments are made in innovation. This is possible through strategies to penetrate the markets further, making improvements in existing products and devising new channels.

6.   Sources of innovative ideas

Where will the innovative ideas come from was the question that was posed to CEO's. The feedback is given below:

Sources	%

- Employees 41
- Business partners 36
- Customers 34
- Consultants 22
- Competitors 20
- Associations/trade shows/conferences 18
- Internal sales and service units 17
- Internal R &D 17
- Academia 13

It is interesting to find that the CEO's believe that most of the innovations will come from within the organization comprising of employees, R & D staff and those from sales & service. Surprisingly, the academia has been given a smaller representation.

7.   Partnering and collaborative benefits

As the costs of innovation will be on the rise, partnering and collaborating with other organizations will become common practice. What are the specific benefits which the CEO's are looking for are given in the table on the next page:

Benefits	%
Reduced costs	42
Higher quality/customer satisfaction	37
Access to skills/products	35
Increased revenue	32
Access to markets/customers	31
Overall speed & strategic flexibility	31
Reduced risk/capital investment	28
Faster time to market	26

- Focus and specialization   25
- Fixed to variable costs   17

While there are number of issues which bring benefits through collaboration, reduction in costs has been more crucial. It is possible to generate a synergy through collaboration which will result in more customer satisfaction to keep one in business.

8.   Obstacles to innovation

The path of innovation is not easy. There are likely to be several obstacles which the organizations are likely to face. They have been identified separately under the headings of External and Internal. The major ones are listed below:

	External	%
•	Government and other legal restrictions	31
•	Economic uncertainty	18
•	Inadequate enabling technologies	15
•	Workforce issues arising externally	11
	Internal	
•	Unsupportive culture and climate	35
•	Limited funding for investment	34
•	Workforce issues	26
•	Process immaturity	23
•	Inflexible physical and IT infrastructure	14
•	Insufficient access to information	12

CEO's will have to instinctively understand the need to play a prominent role in establishing an innovative culture in the organization. A culture which will be collegial and team oriented, but will still reward the individual contributions. It will also have to be more consistent integration of business and technology.

Majority of the CEO's felt that they need to drive fundamental change within their organization within next two years. To achieve this change, innovation is imperative. This again will require a perfect Innovation Mix through proper business models, collaboration and developing the right culture in the organization.

This will be the inescapable responsibility of the CEO's to carve out the future of innovation.

The future of innovation

The IBM study is one of the most detailed studies conducted on the topic of innovation in recent times. Since our actions in the present shape our future, the findings we present above set the stage for the future of innovation.

We explore three topics under the aegis of 'The future of innovation'.

The Global Mind

The findings from the IBM study as well as numerous other studies attest the role of collaboration in driving innovation. Today, collaboration has extended beyond partnerships between different entities such as corporations. Collaboration, with the expansion of the Internet, has extended to all those who intend to collaborate. Any voice can now be heard! For the purpose of the article, we ignore those countless innovations that sprout all around us. We focus on groundbreaking innovations that demand significant resources, and which by their very nature, harbor the capacity to impact our lives in a dramatic manner. Such innovations like the development of the Internet, the proliferation of wireless technology, the decoding of the human genome hold such derivative potential that their discovery can unlock secrets that can transform our lives. For example, several entities have contributed to the success of the Internet- from the engineers who first developed the internet protocol, to the countless companies who built the backbone technology infrastructure that drives the internet to the companies that create the applications that define the Internet we use and touch. Such groundbreaking innovations take several years and participation from a global group of participants – a Global Mind.

Such innovations consume billions of dollars and the brightest minds on the planet. Although individual corporations harbor the potential to conjure such innovations, the prohibitive cost of such innovations and an uncertain path to an unclear future can stall many attempts unless the burden of such attempts can be shared. Information Technology and telecommunications have unlocked our ability to reach minds on any part of our planet. Today, biotechnology labs in San Francisco can partner with labs in Gurgaon, Haryana. The biotech labs in San Francisco can focus on basic research whereas the labs in Haryana can conduct clinical trials, and by the virtue of the cost savings they can drive, can free up crucial investment dollars that can be plowed back into basic research. Such collaboration between 'global minds' can play a critical role in furthering its advances.

Let us look at advances in computational technology – creating computers that can mimic the human brain, can think without the instructions of an operating system and save thousands of times the data that they do today. Such advances require close collaboration between the R&D departments of companies like Intel, Hewlett Packard and academic institutions where professors and their students conduct the research that refines the theoretical base that's so critical to any advances.

Today, physical boundaries cannot arrest or limit innovation's ability to stretch its tentacles. We can connect with anybody, anywhere and anytime. This 'Global Mind' can allow us to discover the best minds to work on ideas. Collaboration portals such as Innovcentive.com allow collaborators to connect with others, solicit help and draw ideas from a 'global mind'. Corporations are realizing that their employees may not always be the best sources for their ideas, and by tapping into virtual communities such as collaboration portals, they can tap into a 'Global Mind' and expand the expertise they need.

Collaboration portals are in the earliest stages of their development. CEOs are slowly waking up to their capabilities. Today, the markets for exchanging and trading ideas are underdeveloped because the three critical parts that will make such 'exchanges' usher-successful are undeveloped. They are the buyers, sellers and the information assets. Buyers of innovative ideas are still scrambling to understand the best sources of ideas. Some companies like Procter & Gamble through their 'Connect and Develop' approach have tapped into a vast global network of people. Most companies will have to adopt such a model in the future, or participate in networks that allow them to connect globally. The most innovative companies in the world will develop the capabilities to tap deeply into the minds of the world, collaborate on them and launch the resulting products or service.

Here's a quick way to see how the future will stretch in front of our eyes: Imagine today how we interact with computers. We primarily interact with the mouse and the keyboard. Today, top companies are exploring all dimensions of human machine interaction that will replicate all forms of human senses such as touch, sight and voice, and they will be able to impart such 'sensory' capabilities on these machines. Such capabilities will further expand the reach to all the global minds there.

Sector Bets

Innovations diffuse in what are defined as 'S' curves. They diffuse slowly along the lower curve of the letter 'S' before they reach an inflection point beyond which the rate of diffusion gathers steam. After running its natural course of life, those innovations give way to new innovations that take off along the lower curve of the letter 'S'. Some innovations also diffuse more rapidly. For example, more people adopted the Internet than the diffusion of the CD player than the television than the radio.

Most innovations are incremental in nature. They drive small advances in existing products or services. For example, televisions with better clarity or more pixels per square inch – an improvement over an existing product, namely, the television. The mother innovation or television was a path breaking innovation. Such innovations are rare.

The last fifty years saw the creation of the television, the personal computer and the Internet. These in turn have spawned industries such as the film industry, the entire computing industry and the entire information industry. Where will the innovators place their bets next? In our opinion, the above industries will still claim some important innovations but sectors such as biotechnology, energy and travel will see serious efforts for game changing innovations. Let's explore why.

The unlocking of the human genome sequence promised to decode the mysteries to several diseases such as cancer, but much remains to be done. As the cost of blockbuster drugs increases to almost $ 1 billion per drug, the large pharmaceutical companies are collaborating with biotechnology companies and their financiers to develop drugs. The biotechnology companies get much needed financing and the large pharmaceutical companies get access to talent and can share the risk with such partners. Portals such an Innovcentive are democratizing access to talent. Started by a group of large pharmaceutical companies, these corporations can post specifications for compounds that they need, and for fees, inventors can profit from the collaboration. Drug development is also seeing frantic activity in the area of 'bio-informatics' where biotechnology meets information technology. Drug development demands advanced computation, mathematical modeling and advanced data mining, and advances in computational technology will only advance drug development. In the near future, technology will be capable of predicting the onset of debilitating diseases much before they show up. Such predictive capability will allow drug companies to focus on preventive medicine rather than just therapeutic medicine.

The planet is running out of oil. The combustion of fossil fuel is releasing tons of carbon dioxide and carbon monoxide into the atmosphere leading to global warming. Green energy has caught the attention of the leading venture capital firms on earth as they have seen the returns from their investments in software and internet startups fade as open source technology has lowered the cost of development. Energy projects demand capital investment in spades. Today, coal based power plants are the cheapest source of energy, but they pollute the atmosphere. China given its hectic pace of launching coal based power plants has now eclipsed the United States as the largest emitter of carbon into the atmosphere. The effects of global warming are all around us, and that has triggered the race to find cleaner and cheaper sources of energy.

Although nuclear energy offers a clean alternative, concerns about the misuse of the related technology to enrich plutonium for the construction of atomic bombs are big hurdles in the widespread proliferation of nuclear based power plants. This changes the focus to other sources of energy such as solar and wind beyond another obvious source i.e. hydroelectric energy. Solar technology is gathering attention. Although it's more expensive per KWH to generate electricity from the sun than from coal, the abundance of sunlight shows more promise than any other potential source of energy. The challenge lies in discovering or inventing cheaper ways to harness the sun's energy and convert photons into electrons. Recently, a solar energy company called Brightsource won contracts with the largest utility company in the state of California to supply solar energy. It's employing a novel approach to generate power. By training mirrors to generate steam by focusing the sun's rays on tanks of water, it's converting solar energy into power. Mirrors or other silicon based devices have low conversion ratios, and efforts on innovation in this area are focused on improving the capabilities of devices to capture solar energy and store it for non-daylight use. The next few decades will see a surge in investments that are focused on improving solar technology. Bio-fuels created from sources such as sugarcane, corn etc also show a lot of promise but their very consumption for use in the creation of bio-fuels is driving up their prices making them economically unviable as compared to petrol (gasoline); also, they don't reduce carbon emissions.

Travel, namely, the automotive sector will see tremendous advances away from the gas powered internal combustion engines which are at the heart of all modern vehicles today. The race is on to develop electric cars that don't run on gasoline, and companies like Better Place are making bold bets on battery technology that can power cars and replace the use of petrol or diesel. This technology is in its infancy but some forecasts note that by 2025 more than 30% of all cars will be electric. If this happens, it will demonstrate a very high rate of diffusion.

Since the above sectors demand large amounts of capital investments, companies will form consortiums to fund and mitigate the risk of potential losses. Governments will partner with private enterprises to bring such technologies to market. For example, the governments of five countries are actively considering launching a network of battery charging stations to help Better Place realize its vision of creating battery powered vehicles. Companies will have to make bold bets; most will fail, but like the information technology giants that have taken centerstage in the past few decades, the future will belong to those who succeed in their efforts – they will be the largest corporations in the world in the next few decades.

The future of innovation lies in our present

The future of innovation lies in the depths of the present. With the recent economic downturn, companies have tightened their R&D spending. Venture capital firms today are interested only in funding incremental innovations that can be sold to larger established firms for the path to an IPO (initial public offering) have dried up. This re-think could derail game changing innovations of the kind we describe above. Innovations are created by a passion for discovery, a sense of adventure and an appetite for risk. If we abandon any of these 'virtues' that make innovation possible, we abandon the ability to create the future. In our present lies the key to the future. If we continue to experiment despite the odds, if we encourage our younger generation to create and not to regurgitate, to think and not to be merely taught to, we will continue to plant the seeds that will bear fruit in the future.

India, if it wants to play a prominent role in the area of innovation in the future, will need to embrace the above virtues. It will have to develop a higher tolerance for experimentation, failure and creative destruction than the exam oriented system of education and low risk 'generic' culture of innovation that's prevalent in corporate India today.

We will leave you with a few lines from Longfellow's immortal poem 'The Psalm of Life':

"Not enjoyment, and not sorrow,

Is our destined end or way?

But to act, that each to-morrow

Find us farther than to-day."

Translation of the word 'act' – experiment and take risks. The future was never created by playing it safe!!

OOO